SPECTRUM

Spelling

Grade 4

McGraw-Hill Children's Publishing

Columbus, Ohio

How to Study a Word

1 Look at the word.

What does it mean?
How is it spelled?
Is it spelled as you expect?
Are there any unusual spellings?

disappear

2 Say the word.

What vowel and consonant sounds
do you hear?
Are there any silent letters?

disappear

3 Think about the word.

How is each sound spelled?
Do you see any familiar word parts?

dis/ap/pear

4 Write the word.

Did you copy all the letters carefully?
Did you think about the sounds
and letters?

disappear

5 Check the spelling.

Did you spell the word correctly?
Do you need to write it again?

disappear

McGraw-Hill
Children's Publishing
A Division of The **McGraw·Hill** Companies

Printed in the United States of America.

Send all inquiries to:
McGraw-Hill Children's Publishing
8787 Orion Place
Columbus, OH 43240-4027

ISBN 1-57768-494-X

1 2 3 4 5 6 7 8 9 10 POH 05 04 03 02 01

Credits
Author: Nancy Roser - Professor, Language and Literacy
Studies
Department of Curriculum and Instruction, The University of
Texas at Austin
Illustrations: Steve McInturff
Electronic Illustrations: Jennie Copeland, Tom Goodwin
Heads: John Kurtz
Handwriting: Theresa Caverly

Contents

1 Spelling the Long a Sound

FOCUS

CORE

1. trail
2. brain
3. stray
4. weight
5. scale
6. paper
7. grain
8. crayon
9. freight
10. brave
11. claim
12. railway
13. erase
14. male
15. paste

Sound	Sign	Spelling
long *a*	/ā/	paper scale claim crayon weight

Say each word. Listen for the long *a* sound.

Study the spelling. How is the long *a* sound spelled in the words *paper, scale, claim, crayon,* and *weight?*

Write the words.

1-6. Write the Core Words in which the long *a* sound is spelled *a* or *a-e*.

7-13. Write the Core Words in which the long *a* sound is spelled *ai* or *ay*.

14-15. Write the Core Words in which the long *a* sound is spelled *eigh*.

16-20. Write the Challenge Words. Circle the letters that spell the long *a* sound.

SPELLING TIP
The long *a* sound can be spelled
a, a-e, ai, ay, and *eigh*.

CHALLENGE

16. chamber
17. neighbor
18. basic
19. agent
20. glacier

Words and Meanings

Write the Core Words that best complete the story.

Freight on the Rails

The first __(1)__ train carried goods instead of people across the country. That train went from California to Maine, stopping at every __(2)__ station in between. It carried almost anything you could imagine, from __(3)__ to feed horses to __(4)__ for writing letters.

At first it was considered so dangerous that women were not allowed to make the run. Only __(5)__ workers could ride on the trains as they clattered along the tracks. Some men and women still __(6)__ that many engineers were killed on the long, lonesome __(7)__ through the wilderness. It took __(8)__ people to run the train in those days. They had to use their __(9)__ power to think their way out of trouble fast.

The most important job was to make sure that not one package would __(10)__ from its route. First, a worker would put each package on a __(11)__ to find its full __(12)__. Then a red __(13)__ was used to mark each label so nobody could __(14)__ it. Next, the worker would __(15)__ the label on the package. Those early days on the tracks were busy ones.

Verb Forms

Study the example. Add *-ed* and *-ing* endings to the Core Words to make new verb forms. You may need to change the spelling of the Core Word when you add the ending.

	-ed	*-ing*
jump	jumped	jumping

16. scale   17. paste   18. claim   19. trail   20. erase

Look and Write Write nine Core Words you find in the pictures below.

1–9.

Make a New Word Change one letter in each of the words below to make one of the Core Words.

10. frail   11. scare   12. brake   13. mate   14. taste   15. weighs

Use the Dictionary Most dictionaries do not include an entry for all forms of every word. To find *pasted* you would have to look up the base word *paste*. Study the How to Use the Dictionary information on pages 104–105. Then write the base word you would look up to find the meaning of each Core Word below.

16. strayed   17. brains   18. erasable   19. freights   20. claiming

Imagine that you are a passenger on a train as it speeds along the track. Write an entry in your journal. Use at least four Core Words from this lesson.

Proofreading practice

1–4. Here is a draft of a journal entry. Find four misspelled words. Write them correctly.

> I am on a train going home It was fun to be on a farm. I can still see the straiy cows and hear the fraight trains. I will always remember how braive I felt when I rode a horse for the first time. It will be hard to erase those good times from my brane

5–6. Two periods were not put at the ends of sentences. Copy the journal entry and correct the spelling and punctuation mistakes.

Now proofread your journal entry and correct any errors.

CORE			CHALLENGE
trail	paper	claim	chamber
brain	grain	railway	neighbor
stray	crayon	erase	basic
weight	freight	male	agent
scale	brave	paste	glacier

2 Spelling the Long *e* Sound

FOCUS

CORE

1. east
2. bleed
3. field
4. donkey
5. sneak
6. jockey
7. grease
8. yield
9. least
10. scream
11. shield
12. wheat
13. seaweed
14. beach
15. beetle

CHALLENGE

16. screech
17. female
18. wreath
19. niece
20. measles

Sound	Sign	Spelling	
long *e*	/ē/	east	bleed
		field	donkey

Say each word. Listen for the long *e* sound.

Study the spelling. How is the long *e* sound spelled in the words *east*, *bleed*, *field*, and *donkey*?

Write the words.

1–8. Write the Core Words in which a long *e* vowel sound is spelled *ea*. Circle two other letters that spell the long *e* sound in the two-syllable word.

9–13. Write the Core Words in which the long *e* sound is spelled *ie* or *ey*.

14–16. Write the Core Words in which the long *e* sound is spelled *ee*.

17–21. Write the Challenge Words. Circle the letters that spell the long *e* sound.

SPELLING TIP
The long *e* sound can be spelled *ee*, *ea*, *ie*, and *ey*.

Words and Meanings

Write the Core Words that best complete the story.

Seaweed Beach

The sun was just rising in the (1). Sina decided to go to the (2) to build a sand castle. She walked past a (3) filled with tall golden stalks of (4). A small (5) sat on top of one of the stalks as if to (6) a look at Sina as she went by.

Sina held her shovel and pail in front of her like a make-believe sword and (7). She pretended to be a knight riding a horse. Though not an experienced rider like a (8), Sina had ridden a little brown (9) many times. She wished for a horse more than anything. But her parents would not (10) to her wish. Well, she could pretend, at (11).

As she got near the water, Sina could smell of heaps of (12). The water was so shiny it looked like oil or (13). She decided to take a short walk along the shore. Suddenly Sina gave a loud (14). She had scraped her foot on a broken seashell, but it didn't (15). Sina forgot all about her cut foot when she got busy building her sand castle.

Compound Words

Study the example. Combine the Core Word with the other word to make a compound word.

sea + weed = seaweed

16. north + east
17. nose + bleed
18. out + field

19. wind + shield
20. battle + field

Break the Code

Each letter of a Core Word is represented by another letter. Use the code to write the Core Words.

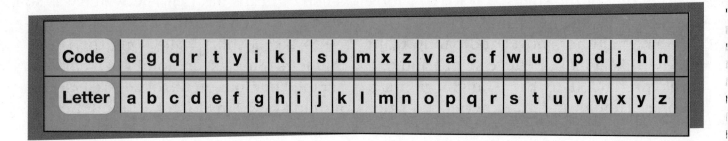

Code	e	g	q	r	t	y	i	k	l	s	b	m	x	z	v	a	c	f	w	u	o	p	d	j	h	n
Letter	a	b	c	d	e	f	g	h	i	j	k	l	m	n	o	p	q	r	s	t	u	v	w	x	y	z

1. yltmr
2. wzteb

3. ftewt
4. wqftex

5. dkteu
6. gteqk

7. mtewu
8. gttumt

9. gmttr
10. svqbth

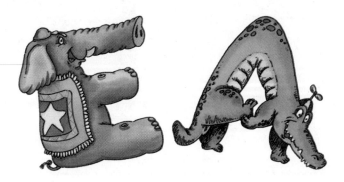

Alphabetize and Write

Write the Core Word that comes in the alphabet between each pair of words.

11. seal,____, second
12. earth,____, easy
13. yesterday,____, young
14. dog,____, down
15. sharp,____, shine

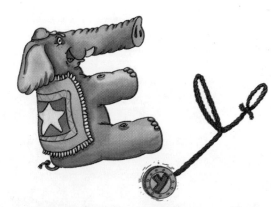

Write a letter to your friend about a day you spent at the beach. Be sure to describe the beach and tell what you did there. Use at least four Core Words from this lesson.

Proofreding praktice

1–3. Here is a draft of part of a letter. Three words are misspelled. Write them correctly.

Dear jenny,
On sunday I went to the beech. There were piles of seeweed everywhere. I spent the day looking for seashells and built at lest four sand castles. I saw a man riding a donkey along the shore. I want to go back again soon.

4–5. Two capital letters were not used at the beginnings of names. Copy the letter and correct the spelling and punctuation errors.

Now proofread your letter and correct any errors.

CORE			CHALLENGE
east	jockey	shield	screech
bleed	grease	wheat	female
field	yield	seaweed	wreath
donkey	least	beach	niece
sneak	scream	beetle	measles

3 Spelling the Long *o* Sound

CORE

1. flow
2. grove
3. throw
4. over
5. shown
6. groan
7. grown
8. stolen
9. hollow
10. coast
11. narrow
12. coach
13. window
14. bowl
15. shadow

Sound	Sign	Spelling	
long *o*	/ō/	over	flow
		grove	groan

Say each word. Listen for the long *o* sound.

Study the spelling. How is the long *o* sound spelled in the words *over*, *flow*, *grove*, and *groan?*

Write the words.

   1–9. Write the Core Words in which the long *o* sound is spelled *ow*.

10–12. Write the Core Words in which the long *o* sound is spelled *o* or *o-e*.

13–15. Write the Core Words in which the long *o* sound is spelled *oa*.

16–20. Write the Challenge Words. Circle the letters that spell the long *o* sound.

SPELLING TIP
The long *o* sound can be spelled *o*, *ow*, *o-e*, and *oa*.

CHALLENGE

16. bulldozer
17. elbow
18. overflow
19. though
20. cocoa

WORDS and MEANINGS

Write the Core Words that best complete the story.

Down the Coast With a Cobra

Long ago a snake charmer traveled down the (1) of India. He rode in a golden (2). During his trip, he saw an orange tree (3) as he looked out the (4). Every so often he would (5) in protest as the wheels went (6) another bump on the (7) road. Sometimes it would even (8) him off his seat!

Next to the man was a basket that held his prize snake. He kept his pet cobra near him because he was afraid that it might be (9). He also had a (10) that people put their money into when they came to see the snake.

Over the years, he had (11) the cobra to people all over India. He would play his (12) flute to charm the snake into rising out of its round home. As it uncoiled, the snake would suddenly blow up its neck, which had now (13) into the shape of a hood. Crowds of people would (14) around the snake that cast such a big (15) in the afternoon sun.

Homophones

Groan and *grown* are homophones. They sound the same but have different spellings and meanings. Write sentences using these homophones.

16. some - sum
17. know - no
18. blue - blew
19. ant - aunt
20. sale - sail

Be an Author Write the Core Word that completes each book title. Be sure to begin each Core Word with a capital letter.

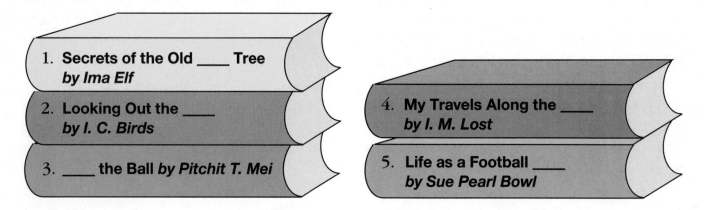

1. Secrets of the Old _____ Tree
   by Ima Elf

2. Looking Out the _____
   by I. C. Birds

3. _____ the Ball *by Pitchit T. Mei*

4. My Travels Along the _____
   by I. M. Lost

5. Life as a Football _____
   by Sue Pearl Bowl

Think and Write Write the Core Word that answers each question.

6. Which word has a double consonant and means the opposite of *wide?*
7. Which word means the opposite of *under?*
8. Which word can be something you put things in or something you do on an alley?
9. Which word can be found in the word *flower?*
10. Which word can be something you ride in or someone who helps a team?

Use the Dictionary A dictionary lists entry words in alphabetical order. If two words have the same first letter, they are alphabetized by their second letters. Sometimes words have to be arranged by looking at the third or fourth letters.

Write each group of Core Words in the order you would find them in the dictionary.

11–13. grown, grove, groan   **14–16.** shadow, stolen, shown

Write an ending to the story about the snake charmer and his cobra. Use at least four Core Words from this lesson.

Proofreding prakticee

Here is a draft of a story ending. Find four misspelled words. Write them correctly.

> The man went back to the coch. He fell asleep on the way to the next town. A shadoe came out from behind a holloe tree. The snake charmer grabbed his bowl of money. He did not want it to be stowlen. All of a sudden a bump woke him up. It was only a dream!

Now proofread your story ending and correct any errors.

CORE			CHALLENGE
flow	groan	narrow	bulldozer
grove	grown	coach	elbow
throw	stolen	window	overflow
over	hollow	bowl	though
shown	coast	shadow	cocoa

4 Spelling the Long *i* Sound

CORE

1. mild
2. pipeline
3. find
4. flight
5. type
6. blind
7. mile
8. midnight
9. idle
10. style
11. pilot
12. mighty
13. supply
14. pirate
15. lighthouse

CHALLENGE

16. hydrant
17. tighten
18. icicle
19. rhyme
20. dynamite

Sound	Sign	Spelling	
long *i*	/ī/	mild	pipeline
		fl**igh**t	type

Say each word. Listen for the long *i* sound.

Study the spelling. How is the long *i* sound spelled in the words *mild, pipeline, flight,* and *type?*

Write the words.

1–6. Write the Core Words in which the long *i* sound is spelled *i.*

7–10. Write the Core Words in which the long *i* sound is spelled *igh.*

11–13. Write the Core Words in which the long *i* sound is spelled *y.*

14–15. Write the Core Words in which the long *i* sound is spelled *i-e.*

16–20. Write the Challenge Words. Circle the letters that spell the long *i* sound.

SPELLING TIP
The long *i* sound can be spelled
i, i-e, igh, and *y.*

Midnight Flight

Write the Core Words that best complete the story.

The (1) climbed into the plane. She knew that a major, (2) storm was blowing up. Although it was after (3) and she was tired, there was no time for her to be (4). She had a long (5) ahead of her.

She was the only one who could (6) the part of the oil (7) where the workers were in trouble. They needed a fresh (8) of medicine in a hurry.

Because of the storm, the pilot would not be able to see the (9) in the harbor, near the sunken (10) ship. She would not be able to see things even one (11) away. She would have to fly (12), using only the instruments on the plane. But she was not the (13) of person to give up. Quitting was not her (14).

The motor of the plane roared to life in the (15), still air. She pushed the throttle forward and taxied out to the runway under the darkness of the gathering clouds.

Prefixes

The prefix *re-* added to the beginning of a word means *again*. Write these words with the prefix *re-*. Then write their new meanings.

16. type
17. order
18. clean

19. lock
20. make

Link and Write Write the Core Word that fits each group of words below.

1. oil, tanker,____
2. noon, clock, time,____
3. flight, airplane, flight attendant,____
4. cabin, cottage, houseboat,____
5. foot, yard, kilometer,____
6. birds, kites, airplanes,____
7. Captain Hook, Long John Silver,____
8. lost, found, lose,____

Match the Keys Write the Core Word that is spelled by matching each key with the correct letter.

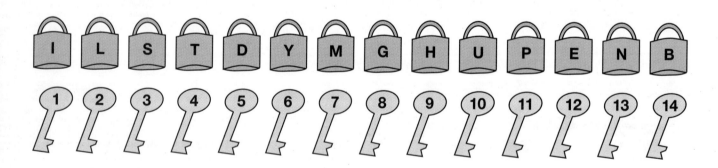

9. 4-6-11-12
10. 7-1-2-5
11. 14-2-1-13-5

12. 3-4-6-2-12
13. 3-10-11-11-2-6

14. 7-1-8-9-4-6
15. 1-5-2-12

Write a help wanted ad for a pilot. Tell some things the pilot must know and be able to do. Use at least four Core Words from this lesson.

Prooofreding prakticee

1–4. Here is a draft of a help wanted ad. Find four misspelled words. Write them correctly.

> HELP WANTED: Pilot to fly the oil pipelyn. Must have at least three years of flite experience. Must know about every tipe of small plane. Will supplie pipeline workers with food and clothing. Good pay and work hours.

Now proofread your help wanted ad and correct any errors.

CORE			CHALLENGE
mild	blind	pilot	hydrant
pipeline	mile	mighty	tighten
find	midnight	supply	icicle
flight	idle	pirate	rhyme
type	style	lighthouse	dynamite

The Review for Lessons 1–4 is found in the Review Section on page 98.

5 Spelling the /ü/ and /ū/ Sounds

CORE

1. rescue
2. few
3. view
4. move
5. due
6. drew
7. proof
8. suit
9. true
10. fruit
11. crew
12. troop
13. juice
14. stoop
15. bruise

CHALLENGE

16. group
17. smooth
18. value
19. issue
20. screwdriver

FOCUS

Sound	Sign	Spelling		
	/ü/	move	true	drew
		proof	suit	juice
long u	/ū/	few	view	rescue

Say each word. Listen for the /ü/ and /ū/ sounds.

Study the spelling. How are the /ü/ and /ū/ sounds spelled in each word?

Write the words.

1–4. Write the Core Words in which the /ü/ sound is spelled *o-e* or *oo*.

5–6. Write the Core Words in which the /ü/ sound is spelled *ew*.

7–13. Write the Core Words in which the /ü/ or /ū/ sound is spelled *ue*, *ui*, or *ui-e*.

14–16. Write the Core Words in which the /ū/ sound is spelled *ue*, *iew*, or *ew*.

17–21. Write the Challenge Words. Circle the letters that spell the /ü/ or /ū/ sound.

SPELLING TIP
The /ü/ sound can be spelled
o-e, ue, ew, oo, ui, and *ui-e.*
The /ū/ sound can be spelled *ew, iew,* and *ue.*

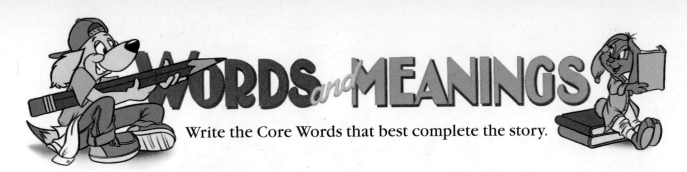

WORDS and MEANINGS

Write the Core Words that best complete the story.

A Giant of a Man

There once was a giant who had to (1) to go under tall trees. Maybe it was not (2), but they say he could (3) faster than lightning. He squeezed a hundred oranges for his breakfast (4) (5). He dressed in logger's clothes and never wore a (6). Although there is no (7) of it, they say he sounded like a whole (8) of elephants when he walked. Birds landed on his head to get a good (9).

There were (10) people on the mountain who did not know the giant. He was famous for coming to the (11) of people in trouble. Some say he did more work himself than a whole (12) of loggers. He did not even get a (13) when a big tree fell on his foot.

The giant (14) respect wherever he went. His legend lives on (15) to his remarkable deeds.

Suffixes

The word *hope* followed by the suffix *-less* means *without hope*. Write a word with the suffix *-less* that matches each definition below.

16. without fear
17. without end
18. without thanks
19. without a clue
20. without care

Pair the Words Write the two Core Words that complete each description.

1–2. People who save other people are called a ____ ____.

3–4. Sometimes in the morning people drink ____ ____.

5–6. A real picture can be called a ____ ____.

Connect the Clues Match each symbol with a clue. Then write the Core Word that fits the clue.

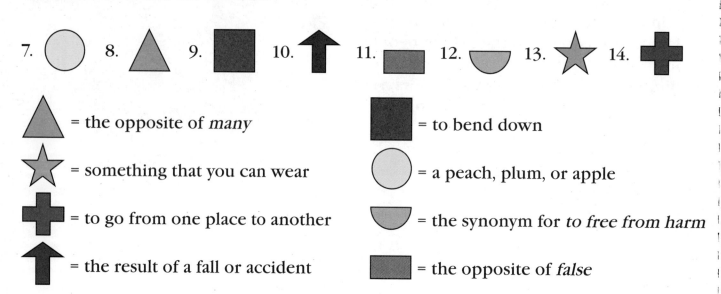

7. ⬤   8. ▲   9. ■   10. ⬆   11. ▬   12. ◠   13. ★   14. ✚

▲ = the opposite of *many*

★ = something that you can wear

✚ = to go from one place to another

⬆ = the result of a fall or accident

■ = to bend down

⬤ = a peach, plum, or apple

◠ = the synonym for *to free from harm*

▬ = the opposite of *false*

Use the Dictionary A dictionary gives the pronunciation of each entry word. Find these pronunciations in your Speller Dictionary. Then write the Core Word for each of these pronunciations.

15. /vū/   **16.** /dü/   **17.** /trüp/   **18.** /prüf/   **19.** /drü/   **20.** /brüz/

Think of a person you would like to interview. Write some questions you would ask in your interview. Use at least four Core Words from this lesson.

Proofreding prakticee

1–4. Here are questions for a logger. Find four misspelled words. Write them correctly.

1. How many people are in your work cru?
2. Did you ever get a bad bruse while working
3. Is it tru that all loggers learn how to rescu people
4. Do you think your job would suit everyone?

5–6. Two question marks were not put in at the ends of questions. Copy the questions and correct all errors.

Now proofread your interview questions and correct any errors.

CORE			CHALLENGE
rescue	drew	crew	group
few	proof	troop	smooth
view	suit	juice	value
move	true	stoop	issue
due	fruit	bruise	screwdriver

6 Spelling the /ou/ and /oi/ Sounds

CORE

1. plow
2. found
3. joint
4. destroy
5. allow
6. ground
7. moist
8. employ
9. tower
10. bounce
11. choice
12. about
13. oyster
14. poison
15. outside

CHALLENGE

16. account
17. appoint
18. enjoyment
19. rejoice
20. trousers

FOCUS

Sound	Spelling	
/ou/	plow	found
/oi/	moist	oyster

Say each word. Listen for the /ou/ sound you hear in *plow* and *found*. Listen for the /oi/ sound you hear in *moist* and *oyster*.

Study the spelling. How is the /ou/ sound spelled in *plow* and *found*? How is the /oi/ sound spelled in *moist* and *oyster*?

Write the words.

1–3. Write the Core Words in which the /ou/ sound is spelled *ow*.

4–8. Write the Core Words in which the /ou/ sound is spelled *ou*.

9–12. Write the Core Words in which the /oi/ sound is spelled *oi*.

13–15. Write the Core Words in which the /oi/ sound is spelled *oy*.

16–20. Write the Challenge Words. Circle the letters that spell the /ou/ or /oi/ sounds.

SPELLING TIP

The /ou/ sound is often spelled *ow* and *ou*. The /oi/ sound is often spelled *oi* and *oy*.

WORDS and MEANINGS

Write the Core Words that best complete the story.

Deep inside its shell the (1) wondered what it was like (2). Would the (3) be all wet and (4) today? If not, the oyster could leave its shell to get some sun. Rain, the oyster felt, was like (5). With luck, the rain would not spoil the oyster's plans today.

Slowly the oyster began to (6) its way up through the sand. It (7) that this was hard to do. Soon it had to (8) all its strength to move ahead. Yet nothing would (9) its hope for a nice sun bath. Little by little it opened the movable (10) of its shell. Now it could (11) itself to see (12) the weather.

The oyster could see a tall building and (13) in the distance. No rain would (14) off the oyster's soft body in this weather! "When it rains," the oyster thought, "I have no (15). I must stay inside my shell and sleep in my shallow water bed."

Words That Show Action Happening Now

Add the ending **-ing** to the words below to show that action is happening now. Write the complete sentences.

16. I am ___ them to come with me. (allow)
17. The air is ___ the plants. (poison)
18. The dog is ___ the rug. (destroy)
19. We are ___ students. (employ)
20. They are ___ the roads. (plow)

Group the Words Write the Core Word that belongs in each word group.

1. damage, ruin, break, _____
2. clam, whale, seal, _____
3. damp, wet, soggy, _____
4. earth, soil, surface, _____
5. let, permit, approve, _____

Answer the Questions Write the Core Words that answer the questions.

6. If you were a farmer, what would you use to get the soil ready?
7. In fairy tales, where are prisoners often kept?
8. When there is more than one way to do something, what do you have?
9. What do some wild mushrooms have that makes them dangerous?
10. What does a ball do?
11. What part of the body connects two parts?

Use the Dictionary Guide words are found at the top of every dictionary page. They show the first and the last entry word on that page. Write the Core Words that you would find on a dictionary page with the guide words listed below.

12. abbreviate/angrily
13. old/oxen
14. cedar/cry
15. fire/fox

Write an ending for the story about the oyster that hated to be moist or write a new ending for a story of your choice. Use at least four Core Words from this lesson.

Proofreding prakticee

1-4. Here is a draft of one student's story ending. Find four misspelled words and write them correctly.

> The oyster had fownd a place for a sun bath. it climbed out of its shell and lay down on the warm ground. Soon it was asleep. When it awoke, it was red and sore. "Wow! the sun can be poisun," the oyster said. "I have a sunburn!" then it jumped into its shell and hurried back to the moyst ocean.

5-6. Three capital letters were not put in at the beginnings of sentences. Copy the story ending and correct all errors.

Now proofread your story ending and correct any errors.

CORE			CHALLENGE
plow	ground	choice	account
found	moist	about	appoint
joint	employ	oyster	enjoyment
destroy	tower	poison	rejoice
allow	bounce	outside	trousers

7 Spelling the /k/ Sound

CORE

1. check
2. lucky
3. plastic
4. pocket
5. picnic
6. struck
7. bucket
8. hockey
9. attic
10. attack
11. jacket
12. stocking
13. rocket
14. shriek
15. ticket

CHALLENGE

16. nickel
17. frantic
18. heroic
19. atomic
20. poetic

FOCUS

Sound	Spelling		
/k/	che**ck**	plasti**c**	shrie**k**

Say each word. Listen for the /k/ sound you hear in *check*, *plastic*, and *shriek*.

Study the spelling. How is the /k/ sound spelled in the words?

Write the words.

  1–11. Write the Core Words in which the /k/ sound is spelled *ck*.

  12–15. Write the Core Words in which the /k/ sound is spelled *c* or *k*. Circle the word in which the /k/ sound is spelled *c* twice.

  16–20. Write the Challenge Words. Circle the letters that spell the /k/ sound in each word.

SPELLING TIP
The /k/ sound can be spelled *c*, *k*, and *ck*.

Words and Meanings

Write the Core Words that best complete the story.

A Wild and Special Friend

I put my (1) to Saturday's big football game in the (2) of my jeans. I grabbed my (3) just in case it got chilly during the game. I packed a (4) lunch to take along. Then I ran upstairs to the (5) where my pet woodchuck lives. He hurt his leg on a fence. Since then he has lived with us in our farmhouse.

Chuckie scares some people, but he would not (6) anybody. He once tore a hole in Mom's (7), but it was a mistake. And he does like to rattle the old milk (8) at night. His favorite toy is a rubber (9) puck. At first he hit it so hard it (10) the window! Chuckie gave such a loud (11) it scared me. He took off like a (12). He caught his foot on a lamp cord and pulled it out of the socket. The lamp fell down but did not break since it was made out of (13). He was (14) not to get hurt.

I did a quick (15) of Chuckie to make sure he was okay. Then I hurried down the stairs to meet my friends at the game.

Adjectives

Words that describe things are called adjectives. The Core Word *lucky* is an adjective. There are many other adjectives that end with *y*. Write an adjective ending with *y* to replace the underlined words.

16. a <u>ridiculous</u> person
17. a(n) <u>raging mad</u> crowd
18. a <u>very attractive</u> flower

19. a <u>bad tempered</u> child
20. a <u>falling</u> or <u>whirling</u> feeling

Make a Connection Write the Core Word that finishes each sentence.

1. *Feet* is to *head* as *basement* is to _____.
2. *Hand* is to *glove* as *body* is to _____.
3. *Money* is to *bank* as *water* is to _____.
4. *Ocean* is to *boat* as *sky* is to _____.
5. *Ball* is to *tennis* as *puck* is to _____.

Write a Rhyme Write the Core Word that rhymes with each underlined word.

6. A doctor who examines near your head does a <u>neck</u> ____.
7. A little spaceship is a <u>pocket</u> ____.
8. A van that has a dent in it is a _____ <u>truck</u>.
9. A little sound is a <u>meek</u> ____.
10. A place to keep a necklace is a <u>locket</u> ____.
11. A pain in your spine is a <u>back</u> ____.
12. A water fowl who wins a game is a ____ <u>ducky</u>.

Give the Answers Write the Core Words that fit the clues.

13–14. Two words that name kinds of clothing
15. The word that names a sport
16. The word that names a part of the house
17. The word that names a kind of noise
18. The word that names an outdoor meal
19. The word that names something that things are made out of
20. The word that names something you need to get into a place

WRITE ON YOUR OWN

Some people have yard sales to raise money for school sports teams. Write a newspaper ad telling what you would like to sell. Try to convince buyers to come. Use at least four Core Words from this lesson in your ad.

Prooofreding prakticee

1–4. Here is a draft of one student's newspaper ad. Find four misspelled words and write them correctly.

Big Yard Sale All Day Friday. Come. Bring your friends. No tickit needed. Save money. Everything from plastik combs to picknic baskets. Some lucky person may go home with a pocket knife, a slightly dented paint buket, a toy rocket, or a hockey stick.

Now proofread your newspaper ad and correct any errors.

CORE			CHALLENGE
check	struck	jacket	nickel
lucky	bucket	stocking	frantic
plastic	hockey	rocket	heroic
pocket	attic	shriek	atomic
picnic	attack	ticket	poetic

8 Spelling the /s/ and /j/ Sounds

CORE

1. ceiling
2. giraffe
3. citizen
4. gem
5. citrus
6. circle
7. cereal
8. genius
9. celery
10. certain
11. gerbil
12. cement
13. center
14. general
15. cedar

CHALLENGE

16. century
17. cymbals
18. genuine
19. cinnamon
20. geography

Sound	Spelling	
/s/	ceiling	citizen
/j/	gem	giraffe

Say each word. Listen for the /s/ sound you hear in *ceiling* and *citizen*. Listen for the /j/ sound you hear in *gem* and *giraffe*.

Study the spelling. How is the /s/ sound spelled in *ceiling* and *citizen?* What letter follows it? How is the /j/ sound spelled in *gem* and *giraffe?* What letter follows it?

Write the words.

1–10. Write the Core Words in which the /s/ sound is spelled *c*. Circle the word that spells the /s/ sound two ways.

11–15. Write the Core Words in which the /j/ sound is spelled *g*.

16–20. Write the Challenge Words. Circle the letters that spell the /s/ and /j/ sounds.

SPELLING TIP

The /s/ sound is spelled *c* before *e* or *i.*
The /j/ sound is spelled *g* before *e* or *i.*

The Man Who Has Everything

Deep in a (1) forest lives a retired army (2) and his little pet (3) in a glass house. His house sparkles like a (4) in the sun. Even the (5) is made of glass. From the (6) of the room he can look up and see the whole sky.

On (7) days it is hot enough to fry eggs on the (8) sidewalk. But he feels as wise as a (9). He built his house taller than a (10) to cool the air. Like a clever fellow, he planned for winter heat, too. In the winter, he trapped heat in a special cell he built in the basement. He planted orange and lemon trees to make (11) drinks all summer long. Nearby, his garden grows tomatoes and (12). He even grows oats for his breakfast (13).

People around here think he is more than a leading (14) of the town. If his friends joined hands, they would form a (15) around the world.

More Than One

Add -s to the ends of the Core Words to write words that mean more than one.

16. one ceiling, three ____
17. one circle, two ____
18. one citizen, four ____
19. one gem, five ____
20. one gerbil, ten ____

Find and Write Write the Core Words that fit the descriptions.

1–2. Two words that name animals
3. A type of fruit tree
4. An evergreen tree known for its good smelling wood
5. Affecting everyone, or an army officer
6. A member of a country
7–8. Two things you eat
9. The word that names a building material
10. The word that names part of a room
11. A closed curved line
12. A valuable rock

Search the Snake Write five Core Words that are hidden in the snake.

13–17.

Use the Dictionary Some words have more than one meaning. Look up the underlined Core Word below in your Speller Dictionary. Write the meaning for the word used in the sentence.

18. Jane stood in the <u>center</u> of the room.
19. The gerbil was the <u>center</u> of attention.
20. Let's go to the shopping <u>center</u>.

Sometimes inventions make life easier. Sometimes inventions can go wrong! Write a story about an invention that did not work. Use at least four Core Words from this lesson.

Prooofreding prakticeе
a   c

1–4. Here is a draft of one student's story. Find four misspelled words and write them correctly.

Sometimes Cesar thought he was a jenius. This time his idea was sertain to work. Today he had built a robot that could spell. But suddenly the robot stopped following his orders The robot spun in a sircle Then it started painting words in the center of the seiling

5–6. Two periods were not put in at the ends of sentences. Copy the story and correct all errors.

Now proofread your story and correct any errors.

CORE			CHALLENGE
ceiling	circle	gerbil	century
giraffe	cereal	cement	cymbals
citizen	genius	center	genuine
gem	celery	general	cinnamon
citrus	certain	cedar	geography

The Review for Lessons 5–8 is found in the Review Section on page 99.

9 Spelling Abbreviations

CORE

1. Dec.
2. Sat.
3. Nov.
4. Mon.
5. Jan.
6. Wed.
7. Apr.
8. Sun.
9. Feb.
10. Thurs.
11. Oct.
12. Aug.
13. Tues.
14. Fri.
15. Mar.

FOCUS

Say the word each abbreviation stands for. Is the abbreviation part of the longer word?

Study the spelling. Look for familiar parts of each name of a month or day. How does each abbreviation begin? How does it end?

Write the words.

1–8. Write the Core Words that are abbreviations for the names of months.

9–15. Write the Core Words that are abbreviations for the names of the days of the week.

16–20. Write the Challenge Words. Circle the abbreviations that do not have vowels.

SPELLING TIP
Abbreviations of months and days begin with capital letters and end with periods.

CHALLENGE

16. St.
17. Blvd.
18. Sept.
19. Ave.
20. Rd.

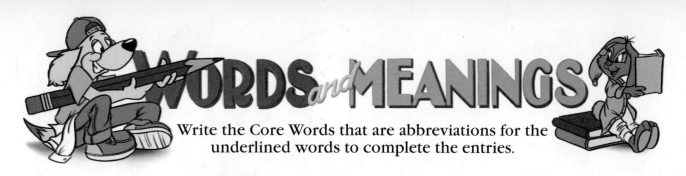

Words and Meanings

Write the Core Words that are abbreviations for the underlined words to complete the entries.

Favorite Diary Entries

(1) Saturday, (2) January 16
I find a dollar in the park.

SATURDAY
JAN. 16
I found a dollar in the park today.

(3) Wednesday, (4) February 24
My brother says I can borrow his bicycle for the whole day.

(5) Friday, (6) March 5
School is called off because of snow.

(7) Monday, (8) April 12
I get A's on my history and my reading tests.

(9) Thursday, (10) August 12
We leave for a vacation in Maine.

(11) Tuesday, (12) October 12
I get to ride in the Columbus Day parade.

(13) Sunday, (14) November 21
We visit grandmother for Thanksgiving.

(15) December
This whole month is full of school parties and holidays. It's the best month of all.

State Abbreviations

The U.S. Postal Service asks everyone to use a two-letter abbreviation for the states. Both letters are capitalized in these abbreviations. Write the abbreviation in the box that stands for each state below.

| NC | IL | AK | MA | AZ | TX | MO | KS | FL |

16. Illinois
17. Massachusetts
18. Texas

19. Missouri
20. Arizona
21. Florida

22. Kansas
23. Arkansas
24. North Carolina

Look into the Words
Write the Core Word hidden in each word. Be sure to use capital letters and periods when you write the abbreviations.

1. decorate
2. sermon
3. wedding
4. octopus
5. unsung
6. Africa
7. submarine
8. satisfy

Write the Date
Use Core Words to write each date.

9. Sunday, January 16
10. Monday, August 24
11. Wednesday, March 3
12. Tuesday, February 16
13. Saturday, April 13
14. Thursday, March 11

Choose the Abbreviation
Write the Core Words that fit the descriptions.

15. Which is the first month of the new year?
16. When do people carve pumpkins for Halloween?
17. In which month do many families get together and give thanks with a big meal?
18. Which is the first day of the week?
19. Which month is known for spring showers?
20. Which is the day before the weekend?

WRITE ON YOUR OWN

Charts can help you keep track of things. Write a chart for jobs at home. Use at least four Core Words from this lesson.

Prooofreding prakticee
a · c

1–6. Here is a draft of one student's chart. Find four misspelled words and two words that need capital letters and write them correctly.

Household Chores for Jon. until apr.			
	clean floor	clear table	wash dishes
Mun.	Sue	Ron	Mike
Tus.	Ron	Sue	Annie
wed.	Mike	Annie	Sue
Thirs.	Annie	Mike	Ron

Now proofread your own chart and correct any errors.

CORE			CHALLENGE
Dec.	Wed.	Oct.	St.
Sat.	Apr.	Aug.	Blvd.
Nov.	Sun.	Tues.	Sept.
Mon.	Feb.	Fri.	Ave.
Jan.	Thurs.	Mar.	Rd.

10 Spelling the /ch/ Sound

FOCUS

CORE

1. ranch
2. stretch
3. pinch
4. scratch
5. perch
6. sketch
7. torch
8. clutch
9. reach
10. hutch
11. couch
12. patch
13. branch
14. watch
15. church

Sound	Spelling	
/ch/	ranch	stretch

Say each word. Listen for the final /ch/ sound you hear in *ranch* and *stretch*.

Study the spelling. How is the /ch/ sound spelled in *ranch?* How is it spelled in *stretch?*

Write the words.

1–8. Write the Core Words in which the /ch/ sound is spelled *ch*.

9–15. Write the Core Words in which the /ch/ sound is spelled *tch*.

16–20. Write the Challenge Words. Circle the letters that spell the /ch/ sound.

SPELLING TIP
The /ch/ sound is often spelled *ch* and *tch*.

CHALLENGE

16. starch
17. cinch
18. patchwork
19. wrench
20. splotch

Pinched and Drenched

I get out of bed and (1) my arms toward the ceiling. The sun looks like a dim (2) as it shines through the clouds. I look out the window as I (3) my head. It looks like rain. Well, the (4) needs a good soaking. The rain will not bother my rabbits in their (5). A look at my (6) tells me it is after noon. My sister is probably downstairs sitting on the (7) drawing a (8) of her favorite horse.

I (9) my towel in my arms and head for the shower. I have to get ready to sing in (10) at the sunset service. I (11) for the soap and feel a sharp (12) on my finger. I look around. My pet bird must be using the shower rod for a (13) again! Cheeper likes being on a shower rod better than on a tree (14) any day. Sure enough, there is Cheeper playing in a (15) of water in the soap dish. I think I will put Cheeper in its cage the next time I take a shower!

Plurals

Add **-es** to each of the Core Words to show more than one. Write each sentence.

16. We will visit two ___. (ranch)
17. There are ___ in the cage. (perch)
18. Who will light the ___? (torch)
19. Both my ___ are broken. (watch)
20. Do three ___ of the farm. (sketch)

Name the Object Write the Core Words that fit the clues.

1. I am a piece of furniture. People sit on me.
   I am a ____.
2. I am a place where cattle live. I have much land.
   I am a ____.
3. I am a part of a tree. Sometimes birds sit on me.
   I am a ____.
4. I can be lit. Sometimes people carry me in the dark.
   I am a ____.
5. I am a place where rabbits live. I am made out of wire and wood.
   I am a ____.
6. I am a drawing. People use pencils or crayons to make me.
   I am a ____.
7. I have numbers and hands. People use me to tell time.
   I am a ____.
8. I am found on pants or shirts. People use me to cover a hole.
   I am a ____.
9. I am a building. Sometimes I have a tall steeple.
   I am a ____.
10. I am a painful squeeze. Some people do it to pennies.
    I am a ____.

Look and Label Write the Core Word that describes what the bird is doing in each picture.

11.   12.   13.   14.   15.

Write a letter to a friend telling about a job that is available on a ranch. Give directions to get to the ranch. Use at least four Core Words from this lesson.

Proofreding prakticee

1–4. Here is a draft of one student's letter. Find four misspelled words and write them correctly.

> Dear Joey,
> Fruit pickers are needed on the rantch. The farm truck will pick up workers at the brach in the road. If you drive, follow Coach Road until you rech the stone chirch. Stay on this road for a stretch, until you see the valley.

Now proofread your letter and correct any errors.

CORE			CHALLENGE
ranch	sketch	couch	starch
stretch	torch	patch	cinch
pinch	clutch	branch	patchwork
scratch	reach	watch	wrench
perch	hutch	church	splotch

11 Spelling Plural Nouns

CORE

1. taxes
2. dollars
3. suitcases
4. monkeys
5. ashes
6. crutches
7. eagles
8. countries
9. bicycles
10. inches
11. sandwiches
12. umbrellas
13. brushes
14. blueberries
15. radishes

CHALLENGE

16. relishes
17. galleries
18. smudges
19. dragonflies
20. marshes

Say each word. Listen for the last sound you hear in each word.

Study the spelling. Are the words singular or plural? What has been added to the singular words to make them mean more than one? Does the spelling of the word ever change when the plural ending is added?

Write the words.

  1–6. Write the Core Words in which *-s* was added to the singular word.

  7–13. Write the Core Words in which *-es* was added to the singular word.

14–15. Write the Core Words in which the final *y* was changed to *i* before adding *-es*.

16–20. Write the Challenge Words. Circle the letters that were changed or added to the word to spell the plural.

SPELLING TIP
Some words form their plural by adding *-s* or *-es*. Words ending with *-y* change *y* to *i* before adding *-es*.

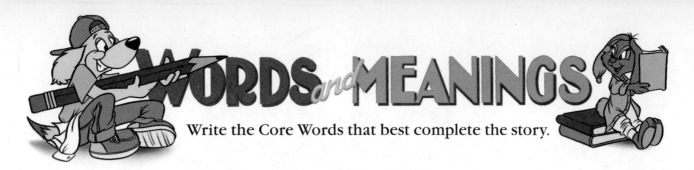

WORDS and MEANINGS

Write the Core Words that best complete the story.

Zoo Attractions

I am lucky to live near a zoo. My friends and I ride our (1) over to see the animals. Some of the animals come from (2) all around the world. My favorite animals are the hairy (3) and the bald (4). We know that some zoos charge an admission fee. But our local zoo is free. It is supported by (5) that the people pay to the city. Our family feels that our (6) are being well spent.

The zoo puts on daily shows for the visitors. People can sit within (7) of animals and watch them do hilarious tricks.

They laugh as some monkeys pretend to be hurt and hobble about on (8). Other monkeys use (9) to fix their hair and rub (10) on their faces as if they were putting on make-up. Some monkeys even carry around (11) as if they were leaving to go on a trip!

When people want to rest in the shade, they can sit at tables with large (12). They can buy peanut butter (13) and bright red (14). And they can order (15) and cream for dessert. A day at the zoo is certainly a fun and busy time!

The Prefix bi-

The **bi-** prefix means "two." A *bicycle* is a cycle with two wheels. Write a definition for each underlined word below. Use the word "two" or "twice" in your definition.

16. a bimonthly meeting of the club
17. a bilingual student from Puerto Rico

18. a set of binoculars for watching birds
19. a biweekly game of chess
20. to bisect a triangle into equal parts

Lesson 11

Write the Plurals Write the Core Word that belongs in each group.

1. pennies, dimes, ____
2. blackberries, grapes, ____
3. lions, seals, ____
4. mops, brooms, ____
5. carrots, beans, ____
6. parrots, bluejays, ____
7. cars, wagons, ____
8. cities, states, ____

Use the Clues Write Core Words for each clue below.

9. It begins with a consonant blend and spells the /ch/ sound *tch.*
10. It begins with a short vowel and rhymes with *flashes.*
11. It has the /k/ sound in the second syllable, but not the letter *k.*
12–13. Two compound words with the vowel sound you hear in *moon*
14–15. Two three-syllable words with double consonants
16. They have *sand* in them, but they are good to eat

Make a Sign Write a Core Word to describe each picture.

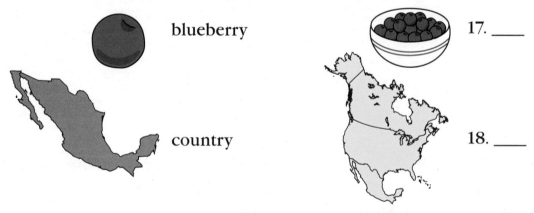

blueberry

17. ____

country

18. ____

Use the Dictionary Some words have more than one part of speech. The dictionary shows this with abbreviations such as *n.* for *noun* and *v.* for *verb.* Look up these words in your Speller Dictionary. Write the parts of speech you find listed for each word.

19. tax   20. inch   21. ash   22. brush

Write a journal entry about a day you just spent at the zoo or another place. You might tell what you liked best. Use at least four Core Words from this lesson.

Proofreding praktice

1–4. Here is a draft of one student's journal entry. Find four misspelled words and write them correctly.

today I went to the Lakeview Zoo with my family. We rode our bicycles there. It cost us two dollers for our family to get in, but it was worth it. I liked the lions, monkies, eagels, and gorillas best. we brought our own sandwhiches, but we bought juice there.

5–6. Two capital letters were not used at the beginnings of sentences. Copy the journal entry and correct all errors.

Now proofread your journal entry and correct any errors.

CORE			CHALLENGE
taxes	crutches	sandwiches	relishes
dollars	eagles	umbrellas	galleries
suitcases	countries	brushes	smudges
monkeys	bicycles	blueberries	dragonflies
ashes	inches	radishes	marshes

12 Spelling the /s/ Sound

CORE

1. chance
2. notice
3. sentence
4. recess
5. price
6. surface
7. prince
8. princess
9. twice
10. office
11. iceberg
12. spice
13. advice
14. faucet
15. spruce

CHALLENGE

16. device
17. science
18. crevice
19. instance
20. distance

FOCUS

Sound	Spelling
/s/	sentence

Say each word. Listen for the two /s/ sounds you hear in *sentence*.

Study the spelling. How is the first /s/ sound spelled in *sentence*? How is it spelled at the end of the word?

Write the words.

  1–6. Write the Core Words with one syllable. Circle the letters that spell the /s/ sound.

  7–15. Write the Core Words that have more than one syllable. Circle the letters that spell the /s/ sound.

  16–20. Write the Challenge Words. Circle the letters that spell the /s/ sound in each word.

SPELLING TIP
The /s/ sound can be spelled *s* or *c*.

Words and Meanings

Write the Core Words that best complete the story.

A Thankful King

The King had a pony that he would not sell at any (1). It added (2) to the King's life. Sometimes it would take a (3) leaping across steep valleys. The King's horses were (4) its size, but it could run faster than any of them.

One day the King and his pony were crossing a river on the royal boat. The boat hit an (5). It was as though a (6) had been turned on. The boat filled with water and began to sink beneath the (7) of the river. The King's helpers quickly tied ropes to a pole made of (8). They put the ropes on the pony's back. It swam to shore, pulling the boat to safety.

"I was given good (9), when I was told to buy this pony," the King told his helpers. "There will be a reward for all of you." Then, after a short (10), the King, the helpers, and the pony returned to the palace.

The next morning, the King called his son, the (11), and his daughter, the (12), into his (13). "I want to issue a (14) to all my subjects," he said. "Write down every (15) I say and post it immediately. From this day, the pony and my helpers who saved my life will be treated royally."

Apostrophes

Rewrite each phrase. Add an apostrophe followed by *s* to show ownership.

For example: "the horses of the King" becomes "the King's horses"

16. the hat of the prince
17. the neck of a pony

18. the job of the helper
19. the side of the boat

20. the gate of the castle

Complete the Comparison Write a Core Word to complete each statement.

1. *One* is to *once* as *two* is to ____.
2. *Water* is to *ice cube* as *ocean* is to ____.
3. *Bucket* is to *pump* as *sink* is to ____.
4. *Work* is to *vacation* as *school* is to ____.
5. *Fish* is to *shark* as *tree* is to ____.
6. *Banana* is to *inside* as *peel* is to ____.
7. *Girl* is to *princess* as *boy* is to ____.

Combine the Parts

8–15. Put these puzzle parts together to make eight Core Words. Not all parts will be used. Some parts will be used more than once.

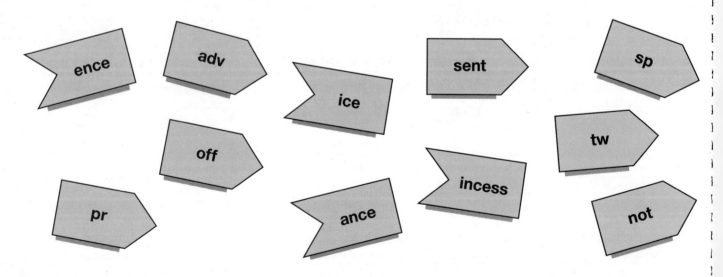

Make a Change Write the Core Words that are formed by changing one letter in each word.

16. change   17. twine   18. spite   19. advise   20. pride

Write a story about another king with a problem. You might tell what the problem is and how the king solves it. Use at least four Core Words from this lesson.

Proofreding prakticee

1-4. Here is a draft of part of one student's story. Find four misspelled words and write them correctly.

All was not well in Frost Kingdom. The iceburg palace was melting. The serface of the ice walls was getting soft. The prince began to notice water on the floor of his ofice. Finally the King took the advise of the Queen. He decided that they would have to make frost.

Now proofread your notice and correct any errors.

CORE			CHALLENGE
chance	surface	iceberg	device
notice	prince	spice	science
sentence	princess	advice	crevice
recess	twice	faucet	instance
price	office	spruce	distance

The Review for Lessons 9–12 is found in the Review Section on page 100.

13 Spelling the /ûr/ Sound

CORE

1. term
2. heard
3. birth
4. word
5. burst
6. world
7. thirst
8. learn
9. serve
10. pearl
11. worst
12. urge
13. worth
14. early
15. further

CHALLENGE

16. search
17. purpose
18. perfect
19. earnest
20. overheard

FOCUS

Sound	Spelling		
/ûr/	term	heard	birth
	word	burst	

Say each word. Listen for the /ûr/ sound you hear in *term*, *heard*, *birth*, *word*, and *burst*.

Study the spelling. How is the /ûr/ sound spelled in each word?

Write the words.

  1–6. Write the Core Words in which the /ûr/ sound is spelled *er* or *ear*.

  7–11. Write the Core Words in which the /ûr/ sound is spelled *ir* or *ur*.

  12–15. Write the Core Words in which the /ûr/ sound is spelled *or*.

  16–20. Write the Challenge Words. Circle the letters that spell the /ûr/ sound.

SPELLING TIP
The /ûr/ sound can be spelled
er, ear, ir, or, or *ur.*

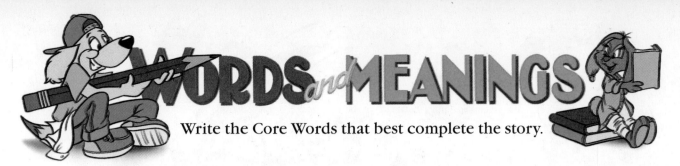

WORDS and MEANINGS

Write the Core Words that best complete the story.

Early Warning System

Sometimes I feel the (1) to visit the garden all alone. The best time is (2) in the morning as the sun comes up. The (3) of a new day is a good time to (4) the garden's secrets. I sit still and watch without saying a single (5). If I get a sudden (6), I fill myself up with fruit juice.

My favorite garden animal is the earthworm. Farmers around the (7) think these animals are (8) their weight in gold. Finding them is like finding a (9) in an oyster! If I watch carefully, I can see its head (10) through the soil as it digs. With (11) study, I learn that the earthworm digs tunnels through the soil. Each tunnel it digs can (12) to prepare the soil for growing plants.

Thunder sends an early warning signal, and I know my (13) of watching is over for the day. When garden animals have no hiding place, their (14) enemy is bad weather. They always run for cover after they have (15) thunder.

Adjectives

Change the nouns to adjectives by adding the ending -*y*. Remember to drop the final *e* before adding *y*. Write each sentence.

16. It was a very ____ speech. (word)
17. This is ____ vegetable soup. (water)
18. I have a ____ dog. (thirst)
19. We like to have ____ teeth. (pearl)
20. Our ____ stew is popular. (spice)

Rhyme and Write Write a Core Word to complete each sentence. The Core Word will rhyme with the underlined word.

1. The loud chirping sound meant we had ____ the bird.
2. A desire to know things is a yearn to ____.
3. When you need water more than ever before it is your worst ____.
4. A strong desire to mix is an ____ to merge.

Break the Code Use the code below to write Core Words.

△ = ear   ● = ir   ▽ = or   ⊗ = st

▢ = ur   ▬ = er   ✳ = th   ▮ = ly

5. f ▢ ✳ ▬

6. b ▢ ⊗

7. b ● ✳

8. s ▬ ve

9. △ ▮

10. w ▽ ✳

11. w ▽ d

12. t ▬ m

Add and Subtract Write the Core Words that are answers to the math problems below.

13. earliest - iest + y =   14. service - ic =   15. clearing - c - ing + n =

Use the Dictionary Write the Core Words that are in the sound spellings below. Use your Speller Dictionary to check your answers.

16. /pûrl/   17. /wûrth/   18. /wûrld/   19. /sûrv/   20. /wûrst/

Earthworms live under the soil. Oysters live underwater.
Pretend you live in one of those places. Write about what
it must be like or how you spend your time. Use at least
four Core Words from this lesson.

Proofreding prakticee

1–4. Here is the draft of one student's description. Find four
misspelled words and write them correctly.

> I had an urge to go exploring in the ocean. I found an oyster
> with a perl inside. It was wurth many dollars. With the
> money I will swim around the wurld to a new underwater
> restaurant I heard of that will surve me the best landfood.

Now proofread your description and correct any errors.

CORE			CHALLENGE
term	world	worst	search
heard	thirst	urge	purpose
birth	learn	worth	perfect
word	serve	early	earnest
burst	pearl	further	overheard

14 Adding -er and -est to Adjectives

CORE

1. hungry
2. happy
3. heaviest
4. prettier
5. uglier
6. prettiest
7. hungriest
8. happier
9. heavier
10. pretty
11. ugliest
12. ugly
13. heavy
14. happiest
15. hungrier

CHALLENGE

16. empty
17. gloomy
18. windy
19. healthy
20. chilly

Base Word	More	Most
hungry	hungrier	hungriest

Say each word. Listen for the final sounds you hear in *hungry*, *hungrier*, and *hungriest*.

Study the spelling. How are the final sounds in *hungry*, *hungrier*, and *hungriest* spelled? How does the spelling of *hungry* change when **-er** and **-est** are added?

Write the words.

1–5. Write the Core Words that end with *y*.

6–10. Write the Core Words to which **-er** has been added.

11–15. Write the Core Words to which **-est** has been added.

16–20. Write the Challenge Words. Circle the letter that spells the last sound in each word.

SPELLING TIP
Adjectives ending in *y* change the *y* to *i* before adding **-er** or **-est**.

WORDS and MEANINGS

Write the Core Words that best complete the story.

Feeling Better Far from Home

The jungle was so hot I wanted to go to sleep. My eyes began to feel as (1) as lead. They felt even (2) than bricks. This was the (3) they had ever felt without closing. An empty feeling told me I was (4), too. In fact, I was getting (5) than a bear. I soon felt that I was the (6) explorer in history.

But I had to admit that it was a nice, (7) day. The sky was the (8) shade of blue I had ever seen. The sparkling waterfalls had never looked (9). Neither had the butterflies that were circling around me. I sat down and looked around for a while.

Suddenly I smiled and felt quite (10) inside. Maybe this was the (11) I had ever felt. Soon my (12) mood made me jump up with joy. Earlier my mood had been sad and (13). The sorrier I felt for myself, the (14) I felt inside. But the (15) feelings cannot last very long when you take the time to look around.

Comparing Words

Add **-er** and **-est** to the words below. Write each word. Be sure to change the *y* to *i* before adding each ending.

16. rainy
17. sunny
18. snowy

19. cloudy
20. funny

Write the Opposite
Write the Core Words that are the opposites of the underlined words.

1. They were so <u>sad</u> to see the ship leave the dock.
2. That is the <u>ugliest</u> hat that I have ever seen.
3. This is the <u>lightest</u> package of all of them.
4. I was much <u>sadder</u> yesterday before I heard the news.
5. The blue coat is <u>prettier</u> than the red one.
6. The books are <u>light</u> to carry.
7. Here is a <u>pretty</u> picture that I made.
8. My jacket is <u>lighter</u> than yours.
9. Who has the <u>prettiest</u> mask?

Fit the Shapes
Use the code to help you write Core Words.

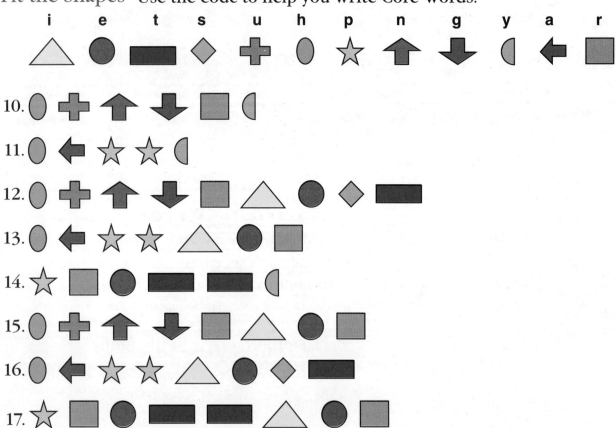

WRITE ON YOUR OWN

Would you like to go exploring in the jungle? Write a journal entry telling about a day in the jungle. Use at least four Core Words from this lesson.

Prooofreding prakticee

1–4. Here is a draft of one student's journal entry. Find four misspelled words and write them correctly.

I heard two ugley elephants fighting One said that she was prettyer. They argued for a long time. After a while the other elephant said that he was the heavyest The other elephant said right now she was the hungryest animal in the jungle!

5–6. Two periods were not put in at the ends of sentences. Copy the journal entry and correct all errors.

Now proofread your journal entry and correct any errors.

CORE			CHALLENGE
hungry	prettiest	ugliest	empty
happy	hungriest	ugly	gloomy
heaviest	happier	heavy	windy
prettier	heavier	happiest	healthy
uglier	pretty	hungrier	chilly

15 Spelling Special Plurals

CORE

1. leaves
2. loaf
3. wolves
4. themselves
5. scarf
6. wives
7. shelves
8. thieves
9. wife
10. thief
11. scarves
12. shelf
13. wolf
14. loaves
15. leaf

CHALLENGE

16. geese
17. dominoes
18. women
19. skis
20. oxen

FOCUS

Singular	Plural
wife	wives
leaf	leaves

Say each word. Listen for the last sounds you hear in *wife* and *wives*, *leaf* and *leaves*.

Study the spelling. How are the last sounds in *wife* and *wives* spelled? How does the spelling of *wife* and *leaf* change when *-es* is added?

Write the words.

  1–7. Write the Core Words that end with *f* or *fe*.

  8–15. Write the Core Words that end with *ves*.

16–20. Write the Challenge Words. Circle the words that end with *-s* or *-es*.

SPELLING TIP

Words ending in *f* or *fe* form plurals by changing the *f* or *fe* to *v* before adding *-es*.

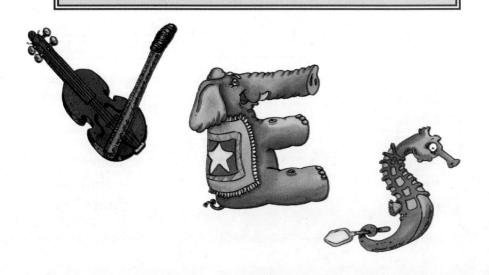

Little Elf Takes a Chance

Once the smallest elf in Fairyland decided to go for a walk. He reached for one last (1) of bread on the top kitchen (2). He needed nothing else from the other kitchen (3). He wrapped the (4) he had taken in a green (5) from a nearby tree.

Out the door he went, taking nobody with him. The other elves had never gone out by (6). They were afraid that a pack of (7) with long teeth might catch them. Or (8) might steal their colorful silk (9). Every husband, (10), and child in Fairyland knew better than to walk alone. Nobody wanted to risk meeting up with a wild (11) or a masked (12). Fairyland (13) always warned their husbands and children to stay together in the forest.

Soon the little elf fell asleep on a bed of green (14). His red silk (15) made a nice blanket. Would the others risk their tiny selves to fetch him home?

Plurals

Some words have unusual plural forms. Complete each sentence with one of the plural nouns below.

children   mice   teeth   men   cacti

16. Most __ can live in dry desert climates.
17. The __ stayed in during recess.
18. My __ will be needing braces.
19. Those __ are with their wives.
20. Many field __ were scurrying around.

Finish the Thought

Write a Core Word to complete each comparison. If the underlined word is singular, your answer should be singular. If the underlined word is plural, your answer should be plural.

1. *Hand* is to <u>glove</u> as *head* is to ____ .
2. *Rewards* are to <u>heroes</u> as *jails* are to ____ .
3. *Man* is to <u>woman</u> as *husband* is to ____ .
4. *Dish* is to <u>cupboard</u> as *book* is to ____ .
5. *Shovel* is to <u>snowflake</u> as *rake* is to ____ .
6. *Our* is to <u>ourselves</u> as *them* is to ____ .
7. *Grapes* are to <u>bunch</u> as *bread* is to ____ .
8. *"Little Red"* is to <u>*"Riding Hood"*</u> as *"Big Bad"* is to ____ .

Count and Write
Write the Core Word that goes with each picture.

9.

10.

11.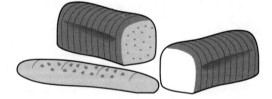

12.

Tell How Many
Write the Core Words that fit the clues.

13. Many people wear them around their necks.
14. A person can buy one at a bakery.
15. The library has books piled on them.
16. Some of these animals are in the woods.
17. There are many in a group of married people.
18. One was sent to prison.

Write an ending for the story about the elf. Tell what happens to him. Use at least four Core Words from this lesson.

Proofreding prakticee

1–4. Here is a draft of one student's story. Find four misspelled words and write them correctly.

> *Little elf was asleep on the leafs when a pack of wolfs woke him up. The elf was frightened. "I'm tired of getting blamed for everything bad that happens," one wolfe told him. "Just to show how nice we are, we will give you two lovs of fresh bread."*

Now proofread your story and correct any errors.

CORE			CHALLENGE
leaves	wives	scarves	geese
loaf	shelves	shelf	dominoes
wolves	thieves	wolf	women
themselves	wife	loaves	skis
scarf	thief	leaf	oxen

16 Spelling Words with the Prefixes *re-* and *un-*

FOCUS

Prefix	Word	New Word
re-	view	review
un-	friendly	unfriendly

Say each word. Listen for the first syllable in *review* and *unfriendly*. The first syllable in each word is a prefix.

Study the spelling. What letters spell the beginning sounds you hear in *review* and *unfriendly*? How does the meaning of the word change when the prefixes *re-* and *un-* are added?

Write the words.

1–8. Write the Core Words that begin with *re-*.

9–15. Write the Core Words that begin with *un-*.

16–20. Write the Challenge Words. Circle the prefix in each word.

SPELLING TIP
The prefix *re-* means *again*.
The prefix *un-* means *not*.

CORE

1. unfriendly
2. review
3. reappear
4. rewind
5. untie
6. remove
7. unhook
8. rename
9. unpaid
10. retake
11. unfair
12. replace
13. uncover
14. rearrange
15. unbeaten

CHALLENGE

16. unplanned
17. refinish
18. unfinished
19. reverse
20. unequal

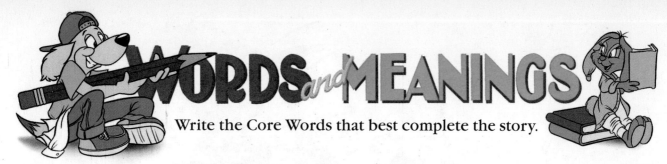

A Magic Show

Who can disappear and suddenly (1) on stage? Who can (2) a handful of scarves with a rabbit? Who can fold and unfold a newspaper to make a fancy umbrella? Who can lift a lid of a box you thought was empty to (3) a ball? Who can (4) balloons into bunches of flowers? Who can (5) a bowl of fish from a little pocket? You guessed it: a magician! Magicians are (6) in their ability to make even an (7) audience laugh.

A magician, whether paid or (8), can charm those who watch the show. The performer may (9) chains or (10) ropes. A magician may (11) a clock or take and (12) photos without using any hands. It almost seems (13) that a magician can do those tricks so easily!

This week they will (14) the Grand Theater. The new name will be the Magic Castle. Tomorrow's newspaper will feature a (15) of the show.

Change the Meaning
Write a word with the **un-** or **re-** prefix that means the following:

16. not common
17. join again
18. not like
19. write again
20. not happy

Listen and List Write the Core Words that fit the descriptions below.

1–5. Five words that have three or more syllables
6–7. Two words that have double consonants
8–12. Five words that have a long vowel sound spelled *a-e* or *ai*

Search and Find Find five Core Words hidden in the puzzle.
Write the words on a separate piece of paper.

13 -17.

```
x u r l i e r e t a k e b
l r e a p p e a r n m y q
o z w e r k t u n h o o k
i t i v o u n f a i r x a
r e n l i e z c c t r l i
l p d l k s d u t r e k m
```

Spell the Answer Write the Core Words that answer the questions.

18. What might you call someone who never smiles or talks to you?
19. What do you do to your laces before you take off your shoes?
20. What do you do when you study for a test?
21. What should you do to a splinter in your finger?
22. What do you call a team that has not lost a game?
23. What do you do when you change the furniture in a room?
24. What do you do about something you need that you have lost or broken?

Write a newspaper review of a magic show. Tell what the magician did and how the audience liked the act. Write a headline for your review. Use at least four Core Words from this lesson.

Proofreding prakticee

1-4. Here is a draft of part of one student's newspaper review. Find four misspelled words and write them correctly.

> Great Night For All
>
> Last night Merlin the Great opened his performance at the
> Magic Castle to an unfrendly audience. But he soon had them
> cheering when he made disappearing things reapear. He was also
> able to unti large knots and remov bunnies from empty hats.

Now proofread your newspaper review and correct any errors.

CORE			CHALLENGE
unfriendly	remove	unfair	unplanned
review	unhook	replace	refinish
reappear	rename	uncover	unfinished
rewind	unpaid	rearrange	reverse
untie	retake	unbeaten	unequal

The Review for Lessons 13–16 is found in the Review Section on page 101.

17 Spelling Homophones

CORE

1. forth
2. flour
3. their
4. foul
5. threw
6. miner
7. waste
8. fowl
9. there
10. minor
11. waist
12. through
13. they're
14. flower
15. fourth

FOCUS

Say each word. Listen for words that sound the same.

Study the spelling. Do the words that sound alike have the same spelling? Do they have the same meaning? These words are called homophones.

Write the words.

1–15. Write the Core Words in homophone groups. Circle the group with three words.

16–20. Write the Challenge Words in homophone groups.

SPELLING TIP

Homophones are words that sound the same but have different spellings and meanings.

CHALLENGE

16. pour
17. principal
18. pore
19. principle
20. poor

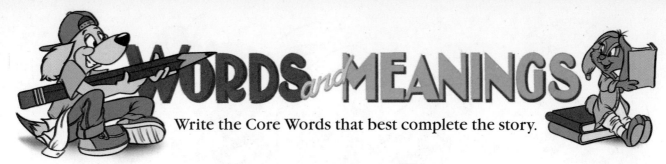

Words and Meanings

Write the Core Words that best complete the story.

Foul Fowl

Long ago lived a rooster known as the (1) (2) because it was not very pleasant. Every morning it crowed at the farmer's window until he came (3) to feed it. Usually that was by the (4) or fifth COCK-A-DOODLE-DO. "I think (5) is no need for that noise," the farmer said. "People need (6) sleep and (7) complaining about you." But the rooster did not care as long as the farmer (8) enough corn on the ground.

This was definitely not a (9) problem. Even the coal (10) down in the valley complained about the noise. One day the farmer said, "I am (11) getting up early to feed you. Tomorrow I will chase you off my farm."

Then the farmer remembered that the rooster chased hungry rabbits out of the (12) gardens. Because of the rooster grain did not go to (13) on the farm. That meant that more grain went to the mill and there was more (14) for the farmer's

bread. The farmer sighed and bowed at the (15). "You are forgiven," he told the rooster. "I will see you again in the morning when you crow!"

Contraction Confusion

Some contractions sound like other words, but their meanings and spellings are very different. Write the correct word to complete these sentences.

16. We must know ____ planning to go. (who's; whose)
17. Try to clean ____ room before leaving. (your; you're)
18. ____ jacket is this? (Who's; Whose)
19. I am happy to know that ____ coming. (your; you're)
20. ____ the book I have been looking for! (Here's; Hears)

Word Play

Rhyme and Write Write the Core Words that rhyme with the words below.

1–2. Two words that rhyme with *new*. Circle the word that is the past tense of *throw*.

3–4. Two words that rhyme with *power*. Circle the word that names something used in cooking.

5–7. Three words that rhyme with *care*. Circle the word that means "belonging to them."

Pick the Word Write the Core Words that fit the clues.

8. someone who works in a mine.
9. something that is less important
  ? minor or miner

10. part of the body
11. poor use
  ? waste or waist

12. a kind of large bird
13. something that is unpleasant
  ? fowl or foul

14. forward
15. after third and before fifth
  ? forth or fourth

Match and Write Write the Core Words that go with the pictures.

16.
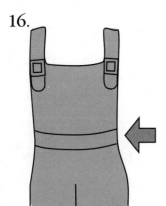

17.

18.
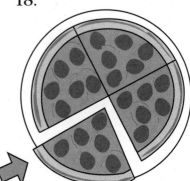

Do you want to help keep the farmer's rooster quiet? Write a letter telling farmers one way to keep a rooster or some other animal quiet. Use at least four Core Words from this lesson.

Proofreding prakticee

1-4. Here is a draft of part of one student's letter. Find four misspelled words and write them correctly.

> I have written a song that will keep your rooster and other farm foul quiet in the morning. You will find their is nothing better. Why waist time with anything else? Just sing it in they're barn each night. They'll sleep until noon. The cost is $129.99.

Now proofread your letter and correct any errors.

CORE			CHALLENGE
forth	miner	waist	pour
flour	waste	through	principal
their	fowl	they're	pore
foul	there	flower	principle
threw	minor	fourth	poor

Spelling the Schwa Sound

CORE

1. woman
2. even
3. kitten
4. bottom
5. custom
6. open
7. person
8. reason
9. happen
10. lesson
11. button
12. garden
13. cannon
14. problem
15. ribbon

Sound	Sign	Spelling
schwa	/ə/	woman even bottom

Say each word. Each word has two syllables. Listen for the unstressed second syllable in *woman*, *even*, and *button*. The vowel sound in the unstressed syllable is called the schwa sound. Note the sign for this sound.

Study the spelling. How is the schwa sound spelled in *woman*, *even*, and *button?*

Write the words.

1–7. Write the Core Words in which the schwa sound is spelled *a* or *e*.

8–15. Write the Core Words in which the schwa sound is spelled *o*.

16–20. Write the Challenge Words. Circle the letter that spells the schwa sound.

SPELLING TIP
The schwa vowel sound appears in many unstressed syllables.
The schwa can be spelled *a, e,* and *o*.

CHALLENGE

16. horizon
17. crimson
18. watermelon
19. dragon
20. opinion

Words and Meanings

Write the Core Words that best complete the story.

A Fool's Friend

The strangest things (1) to me on rainy days. Today it rained and as is my usual (2), everything went wrong. That is the kind of (3) I am. First of all, I woke up late and missed tennis. Next, I had to leave my only clean shirt wide (4) at the top. That is because there was not a single (5) to fasten it with. I could not find a belt, so I had to tie my jeans with a (6). Then I banged my knee on the table. This was not going to be a great day!

I headed downstairs and tripped on the step at the (7). There was no (8) to think that things were going to improve. Why, (9) my pet (10), Fool, was running from me. She is small but she causes a lot of trouble!

With Fool it is always one (11) after another, with knocking things over and such. She also chases around in our flower (12). My brother says she is as dangerous as a loose (13). But Mom thinks having Fool around teaches us a good (14). She says Fool makes us feel better about ourselves. We may have a silly cat, but we have a wise (15) for a mother.

Word Pattern

Write a word for each meaning below. Each word will have two syllables divided between a double consonant. Draw a line between the syllables.

rib/bon   hap/pen

16. a kind of glove
17. sadness or disappointment; it rhymes with borrow

18. the place where you live; 123 Main St., for example
19. 1,000,000
20. a short composition on one topic

Fix the Signs Some letters fell off the signs in Schwaville. Find the word with the missing letters in each sign. Correct it and write the Core Word.

1. **LAUNDRY**
We'll fix your broken _ _ _ ton.

2. **Music School**
Sign up for guitar less_ _.

3. **NURSERY**
Time to start your gard_ _.

4. Free kit_e_ for good home

Think and Spell Write the Core Words that fit the descriptions.

5–11. Seven words that have double consonants
12–14. Three words that end with *-son*
15. The word that has the same vowel sound you hear in *put* and *foot*
16. The word that begins with a consonant blend
17–19. Three words that have a long vowel in the first syllable

Use the Dictionary The entry word in a dictionary is divided into syllables. Find these Core Words in the Speller Dictionary. Write the words and draw a line between the syllables.

20. custom　　21. open　　22. reason　　23. problem

Write a paragraph telling about a very good or very bad day you have had. You might tell how you felt. Use at least four Core Words from this lesson.

Prooofreding a prackticeç c

1–4. Here is the draft of one student's paragraph about a very good day. Find four misspelled words and write them correctly.

> What a great day! the womin who lives next door wanted to give me a gift. It was her way of thanking me for helping in her gardin during summer. she told me to pick out something at the mall. I decided on a little stuffed kittin with a red buttin nose from the toy store.

5–6. Two sentences do not begin with capital letters. Copy the paragraph and correct all errors. Now proofread your own paragraph and correct any errors.

CORE			CHALLENGE
woman	open	button	horizon
even	person	garden	crimson
kitten	reason	cannon	watermelon
bottom	happen	problem	dragon
custom	lesson	ribbon	opinion

19 Spelling Words Ending in -tion, -ture, and -ure

CORE

1. action
2. picture
3. nation
4. creature
5. motion
6. failure
7. mention
8. nature
9. caution
10. furniture
11. location
12. feature
13. condition
14. posture
15. direction

CHALLENGE

16. attention
17. lecture
18. departure
19. creation
20. moisture

Sound	Spelling
/shən/	action
/chər/	picture
/yər/	failure

Say each word. Listen for the last syllable in *action* and *nation*. Listen for the last syllable in *picture* and *creature*. Listen for the last syllable in *failure*.

Study the spelling. How is the /shən/ sound spelled in *action* and *nation*? How is the /chər/ sound spelled in *picture* and *creature*? How is the /yər/ sound spelled in *failure*?

Write the words.

  1–8. Write the Core Words that end with **-tion.**

  9–14. Write the Core Words that end with **-ture.**

  15. Write the Core Word that ends with **-ure.**

16–20. Write the Challenge Words. Circle the last syllable in each word.

SPELLING TIP
The /shən/ sound is often spelled **-tion.**
The /chən/ sound is often spelled **-ture.**
The /yər/ sound is often spelled **-ure.**

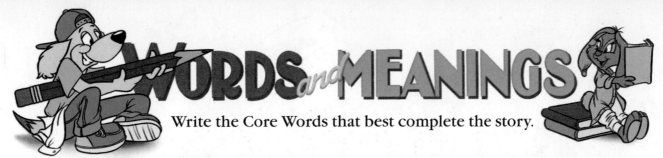

Write the Core Words that best complete the story.

The Most Awful Creature

I asked myself the same question for days. What horrible (1) could I dress up like on Halloween? I could pick something from (2) and the outdoors. Yet a cow would not frighten anybody. It would probably be about as scary as a chair or some other piece of (3)! Or, I could be the most wanted robber in the (4). Scary—that is the (5) I wanted to go in.

But I had the best idea when I saw a (6) in a horror magazine. It was a creature called Dragonking. It was all bent over in a stooping (7). Its arms were making a sweeping (8). Seeing Dragonking in (9) would frighten anyone! Smart people would approach it only with (10).

Unfortunately, the magazine did not (11) the (12) of the shop where the costume could be bought. My friend offered to make a costume like it on the (13) that I help. Each (14) of the face looked really scary. My costume was not going to be a (15). I would be the scariest monster of the night!

Suffixes

The ending *-al* means *like or having the nature of.* Change the nouns to adjectives by adding *-al.* Remember to drop the final *e* before adding *-al.*

16. nature
17. nation
18. condition

19. region
20. practice

Read and Rhyme Write the Core Words that rhyme with the underlined words.

1. I have a <u>notion</u> to stop that ___ .
2. Did I ___ this test will cause a lot of <u>tension</u>?
3. There was a strong <u>reaction</u> to the mayor's ___ .
4. Those horns are a <u>feature</u> of that wild-looking ___ .

Shape the Words Write the Core Words by combining one of the syllables in the shapes. Use the code to help you.

Square: ure pos cau

Triangle: mo fail tion fea

Circle: ture na

5. ■ ●
6. ▲ ●
7. ■ ▲
8. ● ●

9. ● ▲
10. ▲ ■
11. ▲ ▲

Group the Words Write the Core Words that tell about the word groups.

12. birds, flowers, trees, grass
13. Mexico, United States, Egypt, Japan
14. chair, table, couch, bed
15. north, south, east, west
16. healthy, weak, strong, poor
17. place, spot, area, section
18. view, scene, drawing, sketch

Write an ending to the story about Dragonking. Use at least four Core Words from this lesson.

Proofreding prakticee

1-4. Here is a draft of one student's story ending. Find four misspelled words and write them correctly.

> I was dragonking on Halloween night. I went to houses in every directshun in my neighborhood. My efforts were certainly a big fialure! The creture was so scary that nobody would open a door. Next year i will take a different acshon. I will be a cow!

5-6. Two words should have been capitalized. Rewrite the story correcting all errors.

Proofread your story ending and correct any errors.

CORE			CHALLENGE
action	failure	location	attention
picture	mention	feature	lecture
nation	nature	condition	departure
creature	caution	posture	creation
motion	furniture	direction	moisture

20 Spelling Number Words

CORE

1. eighteen
2. twenty
3. thirteen
4. ninety
5. nineteen
6. fifteen
7. million
8. hundred
9. sixteen
10. fifth
11. seventeen
12. fifty
13. eighth
14. fourteen
15. forty

Say each word. Listen for familiar vowel and consonant sounds. Listen for words with the same ending.

Study the spelling. Do you see any familiar long or short vowel spellings? Are there any unusual spellings? Do any of the words have the same endings?

Write the words.

　1–7. Write the Core Words that end with **-teen**.

　8–11. Write the Core Words that end with **-ty**.

12–13. Write the Core Words that end with **-th**.

14–15. Write the Core Words that stand for *100* and *1,000,000*.

16–20. Write the Challenge Words. Circle the words that end with **-al**.

SPELLING TIP

Many number words have expected short and long vowel and consonant spellings.

CHALLENGE

16. numeral
17. digit
18. arithmetic
19. decimal
20. trillion

WORDS and MEANINGS

Write the Core Words that best complete the story.

How Old Is Old?

How old are you now? If you already had your (1) birthday, you would be five years old. Three years later, you would be having your (2) birthday. If you were a teenager, you would have to be (3), (4), (5), (6), (7), (8), or (9). If you were a year older than a teenager, you would be (10). And if you were twice as old as that, you would have to be (11). Ten years later, you would be half a century old at (12). If you then had forty more birthdays, you'd be (13). And ten years later, you would have one (14) candles on your birthday cake. Imagine how large the cake would have to be to hold so many candles.

Of course, you still would not be as old as a dinosaur fossil! Dinosaur bones and footprints can be about two hundred (15) years old.

Number Words

A number that shows the order of things is called an *ordinal* number. Change the following cardinal numbers to ordinal numbers. Add the ending *-th* or *-eth* to each. Remember to change a final *y* to *i* before adding *-th* or *-eth.*

16. fifteen   17. hundred   18. fifty   19. million   20. forty

Name the Numbers Write the Core Words you see on the basketball scoreboard.

1–9.

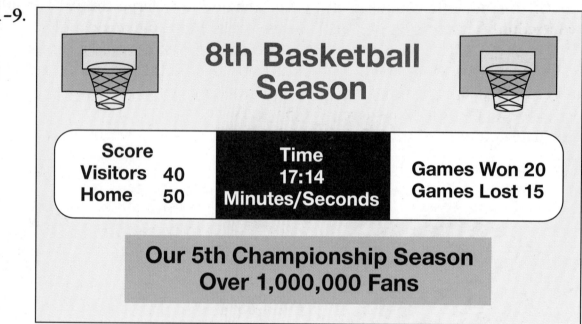

8th Basketball Season

Score		Time	Games Won 20
Visitors	40	17:14	Games Lost 15
Home	50	Minutes/Seconds	

**Our 5th Championship Season
Over 1,000,000 Fans**

Add and Spell Use Core Words to write the answers to the math problems.

10.
$$\begin{array}{r} 6 \\ +7 \\ \hline \end{array}$$

11.
$$\begin{array}{r} 9 \\ +7 \\ \hline \end{array}$$

12.
$$\begin{array}{r} 50 \\ +50 \\ \hline \end{array}$$

13.
$$\begin{array}{r} 10 \\ +10 \\ \hline \end{array}$$

14.
$$\begin{array}{r} 7 \\ +7 \\ \hline \end{array}$$

15.
$$\begin{array}{r} 8 \\ +9 \\ \hline \end{array}$$

16.
$$\begin{array}{r} 40 \\ +50 \\ \hline \end{array}$$

17.
$$\begin{array}{r} 10 \\ +9 \\ \hline \end{array}$$

18.
$$\begin{array}{r} 9 \\ +9 \\ \hline \end{array}$$

19.
$$\begin{array}{r} 25 \\ +25 \\ \hline \end{array}$$

Read the rhyme about numbers. Write a short poem about numbers. Use at least four Core Words from this lesson.

Proofreading praktice

1-4. Here is a draft of one student's poem. Find four misspelled words and write them correctly.

> When I add one to ninteen, I think it is plenty.
> Instead of teens, I am left with twente!
> Thirty, fourty, fivty, sixty,
> I count by tens and think it's nifty.

Now proofread your own poem and correct any errors.

CORE			CHALLENGE
eighteen	fifteen	seventeen	numeral
twenty	million	fifty	digit
thirteen	hundred	eighth	arithmetic
ninety	sixteen	fourteen	decimal
nineteen	fifth	forty	trillion

The Review for Lessons 17–20 is found in the Review Section on page 102.

21 Easily Misspelled Words

FOCUS

CORE

1. another
2. shoe
3. answer
4. sugar
5. young
6. sure
7. obey
8. cousin
9. ocean
10. often
11. guess
12. front
13. wash
14. island
15. whose

Say each word. Listen for familiar vowel and consonant sounds.

Study the spelling. Look for unusual or tricky spellings. Do you see any silent letters? Are some sounds spelled with letters you do not expect?

Write the words.

1–7. Write the Core Words with one syllable. Circle any unusual spellings.

8–14. Write the Core Words with two syllables. Circle any unusual spellings.

15. Write the Core Word with three syllables. Circle any unusual spellings.

16–20. Write the Challenge Words. Circle any unusual spellings.

SPELLING TIP
Some words have unusual spellings that must be remembered.

CHALLENGE

16. heart
17. machine
18. against
19. beauty
20. height

Words and Meanings

Write the Core Words that best complete the story.

Whose Is It?

I live on an (1)____ surrounded by the blue waters of the (2)____. I love exploring with my (3)____, Buddy. Every day we take (4)____ route on our explorations. We are never quite (5)____ what we shall find each time.

Sometimes it is cold out, but more (6)____ it is hot. We dress comfortably and wear a heavy (7)____ to go climbing. We always bring water with us. We use what we do not drink to (8)____ our hot faces and hands.

One day we saw a furry lamb. It was very small, and so it was probably a very (9)____ one. But (10)____ animal was it? We wanted to return the young thing to its owner. We told the lamb to come with us. It was surely born to (11)____! The lamb started to follow us around as if we were sweet as (12)____. The (13)____ to our question was right in (14)____ of our eyes. There was a farmhouse down the road. We went there to bring the lamb back to the rest of the flock. The farmer thanked us. I (15)____ we made both the farmer and the lamb happy!

Prefixes

The prefix **dis-** means *not* or *the opposite of*. Add **dis-** to the underlined words. Write the sentences with their new meanings.

16. Please <u>appear</u> early in the morning.
17. Their tricks will <u>please</u> you.
18. I want you to <u>obey</u> me.
19. Do not <u>trust</u> the other person.

20. We always <u>agree</u> on the answers.
21. I hope she <u>gives</u> the <u>honest</u> answer.
22. The note <u>proves</u> everything.

Make Clue Connections Write the Core Words that fit the clues.

1. There is water all around me but I never swim.
2. I am wet and salty.
3. I am a member of the family.
4. I come after a question.
5. I am what people should do when they see a traffic light.
6. I am what some people do when they do not know an answer.

Spell it Right Write the Core Words that complete the sentences.

7. *High* is to *low* as *old* is to ____.
8. *Hand* is to *glove* as *foot* is to ____.
9. *Floor* is to *sweep* as *dish* is to ____.
10. *Car* is to *road* as *ship* is to ____.
11. *Big* is to *large* as *certain* is to ____.
12. *Top* is to *bottom* as *back* is to ____.
13. *Sour* is to *lemon* as *sweet* is to

Climb and Spell Answer with Core Words.

14–17. Follow the letter trail up the mountain. Along the way find four Core Words. Be careful not to trip over the silent letter in each word.

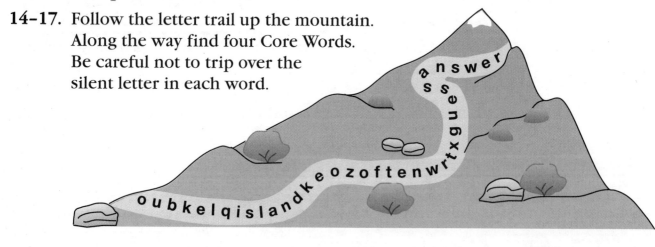

Use the Dictionary Write the Core Words in each group in the order you would find them in your Speller Dictionary.

18–20. often, ocean, obey

21–23. sugar, shoe, sure

24–26. young, whose, wash

27–30. another, answer, often, ocean

84   Lesson 21

Many farmers need help on their farms. Write a help-wanted ad for the newspaper. Tell what the job will be like. Use at least four Core Words from this lesson.

Proofreading practice

1–4. Here is one student's help-wanted ad. Find four misspelled words and write them correctly.

> *Cook Wanted*
>
> *Can be yung or old but must have job experience. Good pay and nice location near the oshun. Time off every week for trips to nearby island. Anser this ad quickly if you are shure you want the job.*

Now proofread your help-wanted ad and correct any errors.

CORE			CHALLENGE
another	sure	guess	heart
shoe	obey	front	machine
answer	cousin	wash	against
sugar	ocean	island	beauty
young	often	whose	height

22 Spelling the Vowel Plus r Sound

FOCUS

CORE

1. glare
2. daring
3. area
4. scare
5. despair
6. library
7. beware
8. swear
9. carry
10. compare
11. therefore
12. repair
13. declare
14. narrate
15. dairy

Sound	Spelling		
/âr/	daring	glare	despair
	swear	therefore	

Say each word. Listen to the vowel plus *r* sounds you hear in *daring, glare, despair, swear,* and *therefore.* Note the sign for this sound.

Study the spelling. How is the /âr/ sound spelled in *daring, glare, despair, swear,* and *therefore?*

Write the words.

1–10. Write the Core Words in which the /âr/ sound is spelled *ar* or *are.*

11–15. Write the Core Words in which the /âr/ sound is spelled *air, ear,* or *ere.*

16–20. Write the Challenge Words. Circle the letters that spell the vowel plus *r* sound.

SPELLING TIP
The /âr/ sound is often spelled *ar, are, air, ear,* and *ere.*

CHALLENGE

16. prepare
17. comparison
18. clarify
19. bury
20. lariat

Words and MEANINGS

Write the Core Words that best complete the story.

Ready for a Whirlwind

According to the radio, we should (1) of the coming storm. Soon someone will (2) an emergency. People here do not get angry and (3) at the radio when they hear a report like this. It does not (4) them too much. This (5) is famous for bad storms. Weather forecasters (6) we have the worst storms in the country. I cannot (7) them with other storms because I have never lived anywhere else. I have not been in many bad storms. (8) I am not as brave or (9) as some people about discussing them. Some people can (10) many a story about scary storms. They tell about the ones they thought might tear down their homes or blow away the cows in the (11).

A tornado can (12) away a home in seconds. Last year one carried off the roof and most of the books inside the town (13). But we do not (14) when we know a storm is coming. We just hope we can (15) the damage.

Word Forms

Change the words by adding the endings below. For some endings, drop the final e. For others, change the *y* to *i* before adding the endings.

16. scare + s =
17. scare + ed =
18. scare + ing =
19. scare + y=

20. scary + er =
21. scary + est =
22. scary+ ness =

Look Them Over Write the Core Words that fit the descriptions.

1-3. Three one-syllable words that rhyme
4-5. Two words with double consonants
6-8. Three words that end with long *e* spelled *y*

Change Places Replace the underlined words in the sentences with the Core Words that have almost the same meaning.

9. We can buy milk at the <u>milk factory</u>.
10. There are good books at the <u>reading place</u>.
11. Will you <u>fix</u> my torn jeans?
12. It is wise to <u>be careful</u> of a strange dog.
13. The make-believe creature can <u>frighten</u> people.
14. If a cat is angry, it might <u>stare angrily</u> at you.
15. What is the <u>amount of surface</u> of the room?
16. Do you <u>promise</u> that everything you say is true?

Go to the Base Write the Core Words that have the same base words as the words below.

17. narrator   18. comparative   19. dared   20. declarative

Pick up the Pieces Write Core Words.

21-25. A tornado has pulled apart five Core Words and scattered their parts. Put two or more parts together to write the five Core Words.

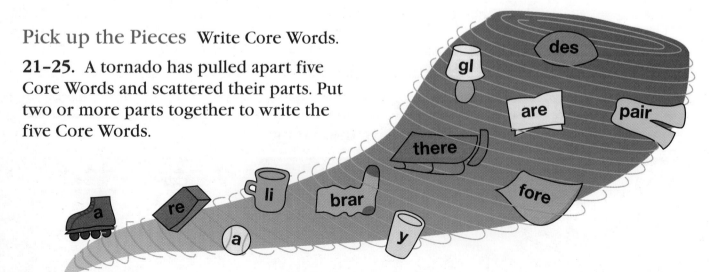

Write a newspaper article giving readers advice on preparing for a storm. You might tell people where they should stay and the things they might need during the storm. Use at least four Core Words from this lesson.

BEWARE! TORNADO IN AREA

Proofreding prakticee

1–4. Here is a draft of one student's article. Find four misspelled words and write them correctly.

A blizzard is coming to this aryea soon. Do not do anything dareing Bewair of high winds and snowdrifts. Make sure you have enough food Have candles or a lantern ready in case the lights go out. Do not let the storm skare you. Prepare ahead!

5–6. Two periods were not put in at the ends of sentences. Copy the article and correct all errors.

Now proofread your newspaper article and correct any errors.

CORE			CHALLENGE
glare	library	therefore	prepare
daring	beware	repair	comparison
area	swear	declare	clarify
scare	carry	narrate	bury
despair	compare	dairy	lariat

23 Spelling Words with the -*ful* and -*less* Suffixes

CORE

1. joyful
2. thankful
3. careful
4. useless
5. hopeful
6. homeless
7. harmful
8. helpless
9. fearful
10. painless
11. painful
12. cloudless
13. playful
14. thankless
15. skillful

Word and Suffix	Meaning
joyful	full of joy
painless	without pain

Say each word. Listen to the last syllable in *joyful*. Listen to the last syllable in *painless*.

Study the spelling. How is the last syllable in *joyful* spelled? How is the last syllable in *painless* spelled? These endings are called suffixes. How does each suffix affect the meaning of the base word?

Write the words.

　　1–9. Write the Core Words that end with -*ful*.

　10–15. Write the Core Words that end with -*less*.

　16–20. Write the Challenge Words. Circle the suffix in each word.

SPELLING TIP
The suffix -*ful* added to a word means *full of*.
The suffix -*less* added to a word means *without*.

CHALLENGE

16. powerful
17. wonderful
18. breathless
19. respectful
20. thoughtful

WORDS and MEANINGS

Write the Core Words that best complete the story.

A Day at the Beach

Yesterday's clouds had disappeared, leaving behind a (1) sky. I was (2) to see that the beach was not crowded. I had been (3) there would be too many people.

I was (4) to put on some lotion as soon as we got there. Once I got a (5), stinging sunburn. I reminded myself that the lotion would be (6) if it washed off when I swam. Without its protection, I would be (7) against the sun's rays. Blocking out the sun in the afternoon will make your evening (8). I told my friends that too much sun can be very (9). It is a (10) job

warning people, though, if they do not believe you.

I felt frisky and (11) as I started to bounce my beach ball. I am (12) at playing ball, but I do like to play with other people. So I was (13) that my friends would play with me. And they did! After a while, we watched the seagulls as they flew around. These (14) creatures live at the beach. It was fun watching them dive into the water to get fish to eat. I felt contented and (15) at the end of a great day at the beach.

Building Words

The *-ful* and *-less* suffixes can be used with many words and endings to make new words. Join the words, suffixes, and endings below to make new words.

16. fear + less =
17. thank + ful =
18. color + ful =

19. cheer + less + ly =
20. hope + ful + ly =

Search and Find Answer with Core Words.

1–6. Use the letters in the beach umbrella to write six Core Words.

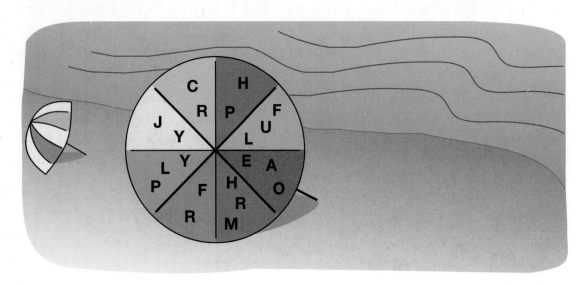

Use the Clues Write a Core Word for each clue.

7–8. Two words in which the long *a* sound is spelled *ai*

9–10. Two words that begin with the same sound as *thick* and *theme*

11. It has the *lp* consonant blend.

12. It has an /ou/ sound spelled *ou*.

13–14. Two words that spell the long *o* sound *o-e*

Use the Dictionary Not all forms of a word are listed as entries in a dictionary. Sometimes you have to look up the base word of words with suffixes. To find *joyfully* you would have to look up *joyful*. Write the entry word you would look up in a dictionary to find information on the words below.

15. carefully   17. panicky   19. homelessness

16. skillfulness   18. playable

Do you like going to the beach? Write a list of rules that should be followed when spending a day at the seashore. Use at least four Core Words from this lesson.

Proofreding prakticee

1–4. Here is one student's list of rules. Find four misspelled words and write them correctly.

Rules for the Beach
1. *Stay out of the harmfull rays of the sun.*
2. *Be carful to throw your trash in garbage cans.*
3. *Do not make usless noise or be too playfal in crowded areas.*
4. *Be fearful of strong ocean currents and tides.*

Now proofread your rules and correct any errors.

CORE			CHALLENGE
joyful	homeless	painful	powerful
thankful	harmful	cloudless	wonderful
careful	helpless	playful	breathless
useless	fearful	thankless	respectful
hopeful	painless	skillful	thoughtful

24 Spelling Words Ending with -ing

CORE

1. swimming
2. dancing
3. napping
4. exploring
5. going
6. snapping
7. building
8. biking
9. relaxing
10. flipping
11. climbing
12. riding
13. reading
14. jogging
15. skiing

CHALLENGE

16. breathing
17. snorkeling
18. practicing
19. vacationing
20. exercising

Word		Ending		Spelling
relax	+	**-ing** =		relaxing
explore	+	**-ing** =		exploring
jog	+	**-ing** =		jogging

Say each word. Listen to the final syllable in *relaxing, jogging,* and *exploring.*

Study the spelling. Does the spelling of the word ever change when **-ing** is added?

Write the words.

1–6. Write the Core Words that did not change when **-ing** was added.

7–10. Write the Core Words in which the final *e* was dropped before adding **-ing**.

11–15. Write the Core Words in which the final consonant was doubled before adding **-ing**.

16–20. Write the Challenge Words. Circle the words that change when adding **-ing**.

SPELLING TIP

Some words do not change when **-ing** is added. When a word ends in *e*, the final *e* is dropped before adding **-ing**. One-syllable words that end with a vowel and consonant double the final consonant before adding **-ing.**

WORDS and MEANINGS

Write the Core Words that best complete the story.

How Will You Spend Your Summer Vacation?

What are you (1) to do on your summer vacation? Many people will be taking it easy and (2) in different ways. Some will spend most of their time (3) in a pool. Others will enjoy (4) through the pages of a magazine or (5) photos of people and sights around them.

Some people like (6) up mountains. Others prefer waiting for winter and (7) down them! Some people enjoy (8) new worlds in the forest or at the seashore.

Some people like moving around. They use horses for (9) and bicycles for (10). Some use their feet for speed walking or (11). When there is music being played, many people go (12).

Of course, some people prefer quietly (13) a book or, if they are sleepy, (14). For a while they spend their time (15) imaginary sand castles and dreaming pictures of what might be.

Another Ending

Change each word below by replacing the *-ing* ending with another ending. Remember to change the spelling of the base word when necessary.

16. surfing - ing + er
17. golfing - ing + ed
18. bowling - ing + er

19. exploring - ing + s
20. flipping - ing + ed

Complete the Sign
The signs below are missing a Core Word. Study the sign and write the missing Core Word.

1.

No __

3.

__ Not Allowed

5.

No __ Allowed

2.

Quiet, __ Room

4.

This Way to Horseback __

6.

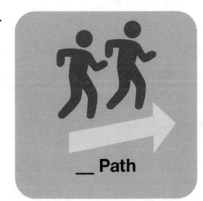

__ Path

Use the Clue
Write the Core Words that fit each clue.

7–9. Words that begin with the consonant blends *sn, fl,* or *cl*
10. Its noun form is *exploration.*
11–12. Two words that have to do with rest and sleep
13. It spells the short *i* sound *ui.*
14. The past tense of this verb is *went.*
15. It rhymes with *prancing.*

Write a letter to a friend telling about the things your family is doing on vacation. Use at least four Core Words from this lesson.

Prooofreding prakticee

1-4. Here is the draft of one student's letter. Find four mispelled words and write them correctly.

We are spending july in Greenfield. My parents are dancing, swimming, and relaxing. My older brother is climbing and biking. My little sister is exploring the beach and bilding sand castles I am going horseback ridding. It is fun being active.

5-6. The writer forgot to capitalize one word and left out a period. Copy the letter and correct all errors.

Now proofread your letter and correct any errors.

CORE			CHALLENGE
swimming	snapping	climbing	breathing
dancing	building	riding	snorkeling
napping	biking	reading	practicing
exploring	relaxing	jogging	vacationing
going	flipping	skiing	exercising

The Review for Lessons 21–24 is found in the Review Section on page 103.

Lessons
1-4

REVIEW

Write a Core Word from Lesson 1 for each clue below. Each word will have the long *a* sound.

1. It tells how heavy you are.
2. A piece of sand
3. The place thoughts come from
4. A soft tool for drawing colored pictures

Write a Core Word from Lesson 2 that fits each group of words. Each word you write will have the long *e* sound.

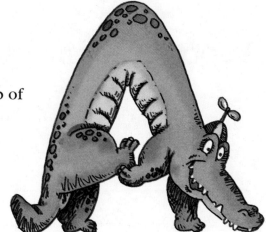

5. corn, beans, oats, ____
6. west, north, south, ____
7. ant, spider, moth, ____
8. cut, scratch, bandage, ____

Write a Core Word from Lesson 3 to complete each sentence. The missing word will rhyme with the underlined word.

9. An empty bird is a ____ <u>swallow</u>.
10. A skinny bow might shoot a ____ <u>arrow</u>.
11. Cooking on a beach is a ____ <u>roast</u>.
12. A pitch from a bird could be a <u>crow</u> ____ .

Rewrite each phrase or sentence below. Replace the underlined word or words with a Core Word from Lesson 4. Each word will have a long *i* sound. The new phrase or sentence is a famous quotation.

13. "Before I judge my neighbor, let me walk a <u>long distance</u> in his moccasins."
    —*SIOUX PROVERB*
14. "He who is most <u>lazy</u>
    Has most of grief." —*EUGENE FITCH WARE*

15. "And... hark! The clock hands wake in fright!
    It is <u>12:00 A.M.</u>" —*ANNETTE ELIZABETH VON DROSTE-HÜLSHOFF*
16. "Three <u>sightless</u> mice, see how they run!"
    —*TRADITIONAL NURSERY RHYME*

REVIEW

Write a Core Word from Lesson 5 to complete each comparison below. The missing word will have the /ū/ or /ü/ sound.

1. *Fiction* is to *fact* as *make-believe* is to ____.
2. *Broccoli* is to *vegetable* as *apple* is to ____.
3. *Eighty* is to *five* as *many* is to ____.
4. *Bill* is to *pay* as *homework* is to ____.

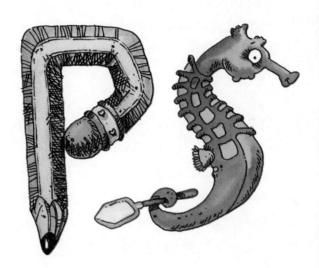

Write a Core Word from Lesson 6 that means the opposite of each word below. The missing word will have an /oi/ or /ou/ sound.

5. dry
6. inside
7. lost
8. forbid

Rewrite each phrase or sentence below. Replace the underlined word or words with a Core Word from Lesson 7. Each word will have a /k/ sound. The corrected phrase or sentence is a famous quotation.

9. "We are so outnumbered there's only one thing to do.
   We must <u>bcgin thc battlc</u>." —SIR ANDREW BROWNE CUNNINGHAM
10. "There was a silence supreme! Not a <u>sudden loud yell</u>,
    not a scream." —LEWIS CARROLL
11. "As he rose like a <u>jet engine</u>, he fell like a stick." —THOMAS PAINE
12. "Hard-boiled as a <u>meal eaten outside egg</u>."
    —EDWARD E. PARAMORE, JR.

Write a Core Word from Lesson 8 that fits each group of words. Each word you write will have the /s/ or /j/ sound.

13. zoo, elephant, tall, neck,
14. morning, breakfast, milk, ____
15. square, triangle, ____
16. floor, walls, ____

Rewrite each note below. Shorten each one by using one or more abbreviations you studied in Lesson 9.

1. The bus will be here on Tuesday, December 4.
2. School will begin in August this year.
3. The club always meets on the first Wednesday.
4. Sunday is the last day of November.

Write a Core Word from Lesson 10 to complete each sentence. The missing word will rhyme with the underlined word and have a /ch/ sound.

5. A bird's nest in a tree might be called a <u>birch</u> ____ .
6. Two small cuts that are the same make a ____ <u>match</u>.
7. If you get a picture and bring it home, you <u>fetch</u> a ____ .
8. A seat that hurts is an <u>ouch</u> ____ .

Write a Core Word from Lesson 11 that fits each group of words. Each word you write will be a plural.

9. hair, paint, tooth, ____
10. nickles, dimes, quarters, ____
11. France, Spain, Canada, ____
12. yards, feet, ____

Rewrite each sentence or phrase below. Replace the underlined word or words with a Core Word from Lesson 12. Each word will have an /s/ sound. The corrected phrase or sentence is a famous quotation.

13. "<u>A suggestion</u> is something the wise don't need and fools won't take.
    —TRADITIONAL PROVERB
14. "He that gives quickly gives <u>two times</u>."
    —MIGUEL DE CERVANTES
15. "Courage is the <u>cost</u> that life exacts for granting peace."
    —AMELIA EARHART PUTNAM
16. "Look beneath the <u>top layer</u>."
    —MARCUS AURELIUS

Write a Core Word from Lesson 13 that is the opposite of the underlined word in the sentence.

1. Kelly arrived too <u>late</u> for the magic show.
2. John wrote the date of George Washington's <u>death</u>.
3. The orange baseball hat looked <u>best</u> on Tonya.
4. Which of the two malls is <u>closer</u>?

Write a Core Word from Lesson 14 to replace the underlined words.

5. Your dog is <u>more hungry</u> than mine.
6. Of all the flowers, the rose is the <u>most pretty</u>.
7. That painting is truly <u>not pleasing to look at</u>.
8. Winning the prize made Julie the <u>most happy</u> person in school.

Rewrite each phrase or sentence below. Replace the underlined word or words with a Core Word from Lesson 15.

9. "Half a <u>chunk of bread</u> is better than none."
   —OLD SAYING
10. " 'Tis like the howling of the Irish <u>wild, dog-like animals</u> against the moon."
    —WILLIAM SHAKESPEARE
11. "He that cries out stop <u>someone who steals</u>, is often he that has stolen the treasure."
    —WILLIAM CONGREVE
12. "The fresh Earth in new <u>green parts of trees</u> dressed."
    —PERCY BYSSHE SHELLEY

Write a Core Word from Lesson 16 that matches each clue.

13. It starts with *re*- and means to put things in a different order.
14. It starts with *un*- and means not playing by the rules.
15. It starts with *un*- and means to undo a shoe.
16. It starts with *re*- and means to look over again.

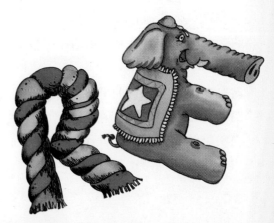

Lessons 17-20 REVIEW

Write the homophone of the word from Lesson 17 in each group that is out of place.

1. chicken, duck, foul, swan,
2. first, second, third, forth
3. flour, daisy, violet, rose
4. middle, waste, body, belt

Rewrite each phrase or sentence below. Replace the underlined word or words with a Core Word from Lesson 18. Each word will have an unstressed schwa or /ə/ sound. The new phrase or sentence is a famous quotation.

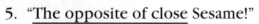

5. "<u>The opposite of close</u> Sesame!"
   —*The Arabian Nights*
6. "There was an old <u>female</u> who lived in a shoe."
   —*Nursery Rhyme*
7. "Mary, Mary, quite contrary, how does your <u>place for raising flowers</u> grow?"
   —*Nursery Rhyme*
8. "The road was a <u>strip of cloth</u> of moonlight."
   —*Alfred Noyes*

Write a Core Word from Lesson 19 for each clue below.

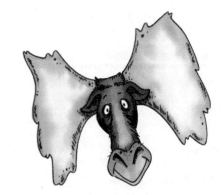

9. something such as a chair or table
10. a country such as Japan or Mexico
11. the opposite of success
12. for example, north or south

Write a Core Word from Lesson 20 that fits each space.

13. thirteen,____, fifteen
14. eighty,____, hundred
15. ____, sixth, seventh
16. ____, ninth, tenth

REVIEW

Lessons 21-24

Write a Core Word from Lesson 21 to complete each sentence. The missing word will rhyme with the underlined word.

1. A medicine that you can count on is a ____ <u>cure</u>.
2. To carry out orders right now is to ____ <u>today</u>.
3. The movement of the sea is the <u>motion</u> of the ____ .
4. A fresh sneaker is a <u>new</u> ____ .

Rewrite each phrase or sentence below. Replace the underlined word or words with a Core Word from Lesson 22. Each word will have a vowel + r sound. The new phrase or sentence is a famous quotation.

5. "<u>Watch out</u> for the Jabberwock, my son!" —LEWIS CARROLL
6. "When I step into this <u>book room</u>, I cannot understand why I ever leave it." —MARIE DE SÉVIGNÉ
7. "O! <u>promise</u> not by the moon." —William Shakespeare
8. "He who has never hoped can never <u>be totally disappointed</u>." —GEORGE BERNARD SHAW

Write a Core Word from Lesson 23 that means the same as each underlined word below. Each word you write will end with *-ful* or *-less*.

9. a <u>clear</u> sky
10. <u>afraid</u> of the dark
11. a <u>cautious</u> person
12. the <u>weak</u> child

Write a Core Word from Lesson 24 by adding *-ing* to each word below.

13. ski
14. nap
15. explore
16. bike

How to Use the Dictionary

The word you look up in a dictionary is called an **entry word**.
A dictionary tells you how to spell and pronounce the word. It also gives one or more definitions for the word.

The entry words in a dictionary are arranged in alphabetical order. If two words have the same first letter, they are put in alphabetical order using the second letter.

Study the dictionary entries below. Notice how much you can learn about a word from a dictionary.

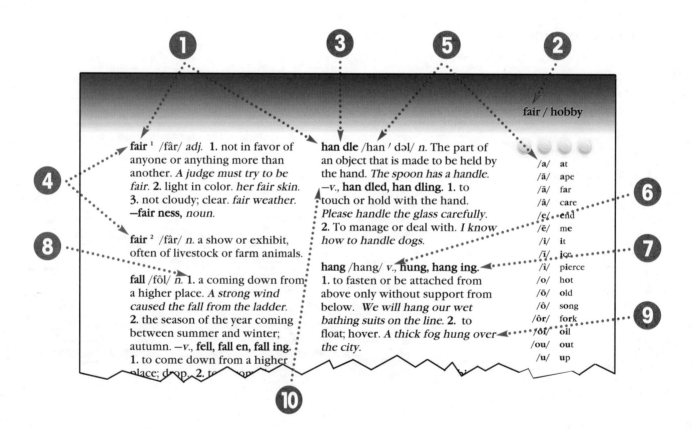

fair / hobby

fair¹ /fâr/ *adj.* **1.** not in favor of anyone or anything more than another. *A judge must try to be fair.* **2.** light in color. *her fair skin.* **3.** not cloudy; clear. *fair weather.* —**fair ness,** *noun.*

fair² /fâr/ *n.* a show or exhibit, often of livestock or farm animals.

fall /fôl/ *n.* **1.** a coming down from a higher place. *A strong wind caused the fall from the ladder.* **2.** the season of the year coming between summer and winter; autumn. —*v.,* **fell, fall en, fall ing. 1.** to come down from a higher place; drop. **2.** t

han dle /han ′ dəl/ *n.* The part of an object that is made to be held by the hand. *The spoon has a handle.* —*v.,* **han dled, han dling. 1.** to touch or hold with the hand. *Please handle the glass carefully.* **2.** To manage or deal with. *I know how to handle dogs.*

hang /hang/ *v.,* **hung, hang ing. 1.** to fasten or be attached from above only without support from below. *We will hang our wet bathing suits on the line.* **2.** to float; hover. *A thick fog hung over the city.*

/a/	at
/ā/	ape
/ä/	far
/â/	care
/e/	end
/ē/	me
/i/	it
/ī/	ice
/î/	pierce
/o/	hot
/ō/	old
/ô/	song
/ôr/	fork
/ôi/	oil
/ou/	out
/u/	up

1 The **entry word** is the word you look up. Entry words are in bold type and listed in alphabetical order.

2 At the top of each dictionary page are two words called **guide words.** They are the first and last entry words appearing on that page. Guide words help you find an entry word quickly.

3 Words with more than one **syllable** are shown in two parts. A space separates the syllables.

4 Sometimes there is more than one entry for a word. When this happens, each entry is numbered.

5 After the entry word is the **pronunciation.** It is given between two lines. Special letters are used to show how to pronounce the word. A **pronunciation key** shows the sound for each special letter. The pronunciation key is found on each page of the dictionary.

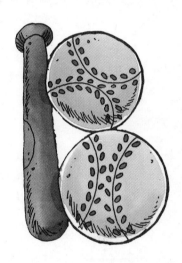

6 An abbreviation for the **part of speech** of the entry word is given after the pronunciation.

7 The dictionary also shows **irregular forms** of the entry word. If an *-s, -es, -ed,* or *-ing* is simply added to the word, the dictionary does not list these regularly spelled forms.

8 One or more **definitions** are given for each entry word. If there is more than one definition, the definitions are numbered.

9 Sometimes the entry word is used in a **sample sentence** or phrase to help explain the meaning of the entry word.

10 Some words can be more than one part of speech. If so, the dictionary sometimes gives another definition for the entry word.

adj.	adjective
adv.	adverb
conj.	conjunction
contr.	contraction
def.	definition
interj.	interjection
n.	noun
pl.	plural
prep.	preposition
pron.	pronoun
sing.	singular
v.	verb
v.i.	intransitive verb
v.t.	transitive verb

Speller Dictionary

· · · A · · · · · · · · · · · ·

a bout /ə bout ʹ/ *prep.* having to do with; concerning. —*adv.* very close to; approximately.

ac count /ə kount ʹ/ *n.* **1.** a spoken or written statement. **2.** a sum of money held in a bank until it is needed.

ac tion /ak ʹ shən/ *n.* **1.** the process of doing something. **2.** something that is done; an act.

ad vice /ad vīs ʹ/ *n.* an idea that is offered to a person about how to solve a problem or how to act in a certain situation; suggestion; recommendation.

a gainst /ə genst ʹ/ *prep.* **1.** in opposition to. **2.** in contact with. *We leaned our bicycles against the building.*

a gent /ā ʹ jənt/ *n.* **1.** a person who acts for some other person or company. **2.** something that produces a certain effect.

al- a suffix that means like; having the nature of. *Natural*

means like nature.

al low /ə low ʹ/ *v.* **1.** to give permission to or for; permit. **2.** to make provision for.

an oth er /ə nuth ʹ ər/ *adj.* **1.** one more; an additional. **2.** a different; some other. —*pron.* **1.** one more; an additional one. **2.** a different person or thing.

an swer /an ʹ sər/ *n.* **1.** something said or written in reply. **2.** the solution to a problem. —*v.* **1.** to speak or write as a reply. **2.** to agree with; match.

an y thing /en ʹ ē thing ʹ/ *pron.* any thing whatever. —*adv.* in any way; at all.

ap point /ə point ʹ/ *v.* **1.** to name or select for a position, office, or duty. **2.** to decide on; set; fix.

Apr. an abbreviation for April.

a re a /âr ʹ ē ə/ *n.* **1.** the amount of surface with a given boundary. **2.** a field of interest, study, or activity.

aren't /ärnt, är ʹ ənt/ *contr.* shortened form of "are not."

a rith me tic /ə rith ′ mə tik/ *n.* addition, subtraction, multiplication, and division.

ash [1] /ash/ *n., pl.* **ash es.** a small amount of grayish white powder left after something has been burned.

ash [2] /ash/ *n., pl.* **ash es.** a tree that has strong wood.

a tom ic /ə tom ′ ik/ *adj.*
1. of or having to do with atoms.
2. using atomic energy.

at tack /ə tak ′/ *n.* the act of attacking. —*v.* to begin to fight against with violence; assault.

at ten tion /ə ten ′ shən/ *n.* watching, listening, concentrating.

at tic /at ′ ik/ *n.* the space just below the roof of a house.

Aug. an abbreviation for August.

Ave. an abbreviation for *Avenue* used in a written address.

a way /ə wā ′/ *adv.* **1.** from this or that place. **2.** at a distance. **3.** in another direction; aside. **4.** from or out of one's possession or use. **5.** out of existence. *The sound of footsteps faded away.* **6.** without interruption; continuously. —*adj.* **1.** distant. **2.** absent; gone.

··· B ········ B ····

bak er /bā ′ kər/ *n.* a person who bakes and sells baked items.

ba sic /bā ′ sik/ *adj.* forming the most important part; fundamental.

beach /bēch/ *n., pl.* **beach es.** the land along the edge of an ocean or other body of water. —*v.* to run a boat onto a beach.

bear [1] /bâr/ *n.* a large, heavy animal with thick, shaggy fur.

bear [2] /bâr/ *v.* **bore, borne,** or **born, bear ing.** to hold up; support or carry.

beau ty /bū ′ tē/ *n., pl.* **beau ties.** a quality that makes a person or thing beautiful.

bee tle /bē ′ təl/ *n.* an insect with hard front wings that cover the hind wings when they are folded.

be ware /bi wâr ′/ *v.* to be on one'sguard; be careful.

bi- a prefix that means having or involving two. *Bilevel means having two levels.*

bi cy cle /bī ′ si kəl/ *n., pl.* **bi cy cles.** a light vehicle with two wheels, one behind the other.

/a/	at
/ā/	ape
/ä/	far
/â/	care
/e/	end
/ē/	me
/i/	it
/ī/	ice
/i/	pierce
/o/	hot
/ō/	old
/ô/	song
/ôr/	fork
/oi/	oil
/ou/	out
/u/	up
/ū/	use
/ü/	rule
/u/	pull
/ûr/	turn
/ch/	chin
/ng/	sing
/sh/	shop
/th/	thin
/th/	this
/hw/	white
/zh/	treasure
/ə/	about
	taken
	pencil
	lemon
	circus

bike /bīk/ *n.* a bicycle. —*v.* **biked, bik ing.** to ride a bicycle.

birth /bûrth/ *n.* **1.** the time when a person or animal first comes from its mother. **2.** the start of something; beginning.

birth day /bûrth ′ dā/*n.* the day on which a person is born.

bite /bīt/ *v.* **bit, bit ten** or **bit, bit ing. 1.** to seize, cut into, or pierce with the teeth. **2.** to make something sting. **3.** to take or swallow bait. —*n.* **1.** a seizing or cutting into something with the teeth. **2.** a wound made by biting. **3.** a piece bitten off. **4.** to take or swallow bait.

bleed /blēd/ *v.* **bled, bleed ing. 1.** to lose blood. **2.** to lose sap or other liquid. *The tree will bleed if you cut into its trunk.*

blind /blīnd/ *n.* something that blocks a person's sight or keeps the lights out. —*v.* **1.** to make unable to see. **2.** to take away thought or good judgment. —*adj.* **1.** without sight. **2.** hidden; not easily seen.

blue ber ry /blü ′ ber ′ ē/ *n., pl.* **blue ber ries.** a small, dark, blue, sweet berry with tiny seeds.

Blvd. an abbreviation for *Boulevard* used in a written address.

bot tom /bot ′ əm/ *n.* **1.** the lowest part. **2.** the under or lower part. **3.** the ground under a body of water. **4.** the most important part; basis. —*adj.* lowest or last.

bounce /bouns/ *v.* to spring back or up after hitting something.

bowl /bōl/ *n.* a rounded dish. —*v.* to roll a ball in bowling.

box [1] /boks/ *n., pl.* **box es. 1.** a stiff container, usually having four sides, a bottom, and a cover. **2.** a closed-in area.

box [2] /boks/ *n., pl.* **box es.** a blow made with the open hand or fist.—*v.* to hit with the open hand or fist.

brain /brān/ *n.* **1.** the large mass of nerve tissue that is inside the skull of persons and animals. It is the main part of the nervous system and controls the actions of the body. It is also the center of thought, memory, learning, and emotions. **2.** intelligence. —*v.* to hit on the head.

branch /branch/ *n., pl.* **branch es. 1.** a part of a tree or bush that grows out from the trunk. **2.** a division, office, or part of a large thing. —*v.* to divide into branches.

brave /brāv/ *adj.* having courage. —*v.* **braved, brav ing.** to face danger or pain without being overcome by fear.

breathe /brēth/ *v.* **breathed, breath ing.** to draw air into the lungs and then release it.

breath less /breth ′ lis/ *adj.* out of breath. —**breath less ly,** *adv.*—**breath less ness,** *n.*

broil /broil/ *v.* **1.** to cook over an open fire or under the flame in the broiler of a stove. **2.** to be or make very hot.

bruise /brüz/ *n.* **1.** an injury that makes a bluish or blackish mark on the skin. **2.** a mark on a fruit, vegetable, or plant caused by a blow or bump. —*v.* to cause a bruise on the skin of.

brush [1] /brush/ *n., pl.* **brush es. 1.** a tool used for scrubbing, smoothing, sweeping, or painting. **2.** light touches in passing. —*v.* **1.** to use a brush on. **2.** to remove with a brush.

brush [2] /brush/ *n., pl.* **brush es. 1.** shrubs, small trees, and bushes growing together. **2.** twigs or branches cut or broken off from trees.

buck et /buk ′ it/ *n.* a sturdy container with a round, open top and a flat bottom; pail.

build /bild/ *v.* **built, build ing. 1.** to make by putting parts or materials together. **2.** to form little by little; develop. *build a successful business.*

bull do zer /bùl dō ′ zər/ *n.* a tractor with a powerful motor and a heavy metal blade in front. Bulldozers are used for clearing land by moving earth and rocks.

burn /bûrn/ *v.* **burned** or **burnt, burn ing. 1.** to set on fire; be on fire. **2.** to injure by certain rays, like those of the sun. **3.** to use as a fuel. —*n.* an injury caused by fire or heat.

burst /bûrst/ *v.* **1.** to break open suddenly. **2.** to be very full. **3.** to come or go suddenly. **4.** to show strong emotion suddenly. —*n.* **1.** the act of bursting; outbreak. **2.** a sudden effort.

bur y /ber ′ ē, bâr ′ ē/ *v.* **bur ied, bur y ing. 1.** to put in the earth, a tomb, or the sea. **2.** to cover up; hide.

but ton /but ′ ən/ *n.* **1.** a small, round, flat thing that is used to fasten clothing or to ornament it. **2.** a knob or disk that is turned or pushed to make something work. —*v.* to fasten with buttons.

buy /bī/ *v.* **bought, buy ing.** to get something by paying money for it.—*n.* something offered for sale at a low price; bargain.

…C…………………

calf /kaf/ *n., pl.* **calves.** a young cow, seal, elephant, or whale.

/a/ at
/ā/ ape
/ä/ far
/â/ care
/e/ end
/ē/ me
/i/ it
/ī/ ice
/i/ pierce
/o/ hot
/ō/ old
/ô/ song
/ôr/ fork
/oi/ oil
/ou/ out
/u/ up
/ū/ use
/ü/ rule
/u/ pull
/ûr/ turn
/ch/ chin
/ng/ sing
/sh/ shop
/th/ thin
/th/ this
/hw/ white
/zh/ treasure
/ə/ about
    taken
    pencil
    lemon
    circus

adj.	adjective
adv.	adverb
conj.	conjunction
contr.	contraction
def.	definition
interj.	interjection
n.	noun
pl.	plural
prep.	preposition
pron.	pronoun
sing.	singular
v.	verb
v.i.	intransitive verb
v.t.	transitive verb

can non /kan ˈ ən/ *n., pl.*
can nons or **can non.** a large
heavy gun that is mounted on
wheels or some other base.

care ful /kâr ˈ fəl/ *adj.* paying
close attention; watchful.
—**care ful ly,** *adv.*
—**care ful ness,** *n.*

car ry /kar ˈ ē, kâr ˈ ē/ *v.*
car ried, car ry ing. 1. to
move from one place to another. **2.** to have something.
3. to keep doing something.
4. to move a number from one
column or place and add it to
another.

catch /kach/ *v.* **caught,**
catch ing. 1. to take or get hold
of something or someone that is
moving. **2.** to be in time for.
3. to become hooked or fastened. **4.** to surprise. **5.** to get;
receive. —*n., pl.* **catch es. 1.** the
act of catching something or
someone. **2.** a game in which a
ball is thrown back and forth.

cau tion /kô ˈ shən/ *n.* close
care; watchfulness. —*v.* to warn.

ce dar /sē ˈ dər/ *n.* an evergreen
that has needle-shaped leaves.

ceil ing /sē ˈ ling/ *n.* **1.** the
inside overhead surface of a
room. **2.** upper limit.

cel er y /sel ˈ ə rē/ *n.* the crisp
green or cream-colored stalks of
a plant that is also called celery.
The stalks are eaten raw or
cooked.

ce ment /sə ment ˈ/ *n.* **1.** a powder made by burning a mixture
of limestone and clay. **2.** any
soft, sticky substance that hard-
ens to hold things together. —*v.*
1. to fasten with cement. **2.** to
make firm or secure.

cen ter /sen ˈ tər/ *n.* **1.** the middle point, part, or place of something. **2.** a main person, place,
or thing. —*v.* to put in or at the
center.

cen tral /sen ˈ trəl/ *adj.* **1.** in, at,
or near the center or middle.
2. very important.

cen tur y /sen ˈ chə rē/ *n., pl.*
cen tu ries. a period of one
hundred years.

ce re al /sir ˈ ē əl/ *n.* **1.** any
grass whose grains are used for
food. Wheat, oats, rye, barley,
and rice are cereals. **2.** a food
that is made from this grain,
such as oatmeal.

cer tain /sûr ˈ tən/ *adj.* **1.** sure;
positive. **2.** some; particular.

chair /châr/ *n.* **1.** a piece of furniture for one person to sit on.
2. a chairperson.

cham ber /chām ˈ bər/ *n.* **1.** a
room in a house or other building. **2.** the office of a judge, usually in a courthouse. **3.** a hall
where a lawmaking body meets.
4. a legislature or other group of
lawmakers. **5.** an enclosed space
in the body of an animal or
plant. **6.** the part of the barrel of

a gun into which a shell is put.

chance /chans/ *n.* **1.** a good or favorable opportunity. **2.** a risk. —*v.* **chanced, chanc ing.** to risk. —*adj.* not expected or planned; accidental.

check /chek/ *n.* a test or other way of finding out if something is correct or as it should be. —*v.* to test or compare to find out if something is correct or as it should be.

chew /chü/ *v.* **1.** to crush and grind something with the teeth. **2.** to make by chewing.

child /chīld/ *n., pl.* **chil dren. 1.** a son or daughter. **2.** a young boy or girl. **3.** a baby; infant.

chil dren /chil ′ drən/ *n.* the plural of child.

chill y /chil ′ ē/ *adj.* **chill i er, chill i est.** unpleasantly cold; not warm and friendly.

choice /chois/ *n.* **1.** the act or result of choosing. **2.** the chance to choose. —*adj.* of very good quality; excellent.

choose /chüz/ *v.* **chose, cho sen, choos ing. 1.** to select one or more from all that are available. **2.** to decide or prefer to do something.

church /chûrch/ *n., pl.* **church es. 1.** a building where people gather together for Christian worship. **2.** a group

of Christians having the same beliefs; denomination.

cinch /sinch/ *n., pl.* **cinch es. 1.** a strap used on a horse. **2.** *Slang.* something sure or easy. —*v.* **1.** to bind firmly. **2.** *Slang.* to make sure of.

cin na mon /sin ′ ə mən/ *n.* **1.** a reddish brown spice. **2.** a light, reddish brown color. —*adj.* having a light, reddish brown color.

cir cle /sûr kəl/ *n.* **1.** a closed curved line made up of points that are all the same distance from a point inside called the center. **2.** anything that is shaped like a circle. —*v.* to make a circle around.

cir cus /sûr ′ kəs/ *n., pl.* **cir cus es.** a show with trained animals and people who entertain.

cit i zen /sit ′ ə zən/ *n.* **1.** a person who was born in a country or who chooses to live in and become a member of a country. **2.** any person who lives in a town or city.

cit rus /sit ′ rəs/ *adj.* having to do with a group of trees whose fruits are juicy and often have a thick rind. Oranges, grapefruits, lemons, and limes are citrus fruits.

cit y /sit ′ ē/ *n.* a large area where many people live and work.

/a/	at
/ā/	ape
/ä/	far
/â/	care
/e/	end
/ē/	me
/i/	it
/ī/	ice
/î/	pierce
/o/	hot
/ō/	old
/ô/	song
/ôr/	fork
/oi/	oil
/ou/	out
/u/	up
/ū/	use
/ü/	rule
/ù/	pull
/ûr/	turn
/ch/	chin
/ng/	sing
/sh/	shop
/th/	thin
/th/	this
/hw/	white
/zh/	treasure
/ə/	about
	taken
	pencil
	lemon
	circus

111

adj.	adjective
adv.	adverb
conj.	conjunction
contr.	contraction
def.	definition
interj.	interjection
n.	noun
pl.	plural
prep.	preposition
pron.	pronoun
sing.	singular
v.	verb
v.i.	intransitive verb
v.t.	transitive verb

claim /klām/ *n.* **1.** a demand for something as one's right. **2.** a statement that something is true. —*v.* **1.** to declare or take as one's own. **2.** to say that something is true.

clar i fy /klar ′ ə fī ′, klâr ə fī ′/ *v.* **clar i fied, clar i fy ing.** to make something easier to understand.

clean /klēn/ *adj.* **1.** free from dirt. **2.** honorable or fair. **3.** complete; thorough. —*adv.* completely. —*v.* to make clean.

climb /klīm/ *v.* **climb ing.** **1.** to move upward using the hands and feet. **2.** to go steadily upward; rise. —*n.* the act of climbing.

cloud less /kloud ′ lis/ *adj.* without clouds; clear; bright. —**cloud less ly,** *adv.* —**cloud less ness,** *n.*

clutch /kluch/ *n., pl.* **clutch es.** **1.** a tight grasp. **2.** a device in a machine that connects or disconnects the motor. —*v.* to grasp tightly.

coach /kōch/ *n., pl.* **coach es.** **1.** a large closed carriage pulled by horses. **2.** a teacher or trainer of athletes. —*v.* to teach or train.

coast /kōst/ *n.* the land next to the sea; seashore. —*v.* to ride or slide along without effort or power.

co coa /kō ′ kō/ *n.* a brown powder that tastes like chocolate. Cocoa is made by grinding the dried seeds of the cacao tree and removing the fat. **2.** a drink made by mixing cocoa powder, sugar, and milk or water.

coin /koin/ *n.* a piece of metal used as money. —*v.* **1.** to make money by stamping metal. **2.** to invent.

col or /kul ′ ər/ *n.* a quality of light as we see it with our eyes. —*v.* to give color to.

com pare /kəm pâr ′/ *v.* **com pared, com par ing.** to say or think that something is like something else.

com par i son /kəm par ′ ə sən, kəm pâr ′ ə sən/ *n.* finding likenesses and differences between persons or things.

con di tion /kən dish ′ ən/ *n.* **1.** the way that a person or thing is. **2.** a state of a part of the body. *heart condition.* **3.** something required. —*v.* **1.** to put in a healthy state or good shape. **2.** to become accustomed to something.

couch /kouch/ *n., pl.* **couch es.** a piece of furniture that two or more people can sit on at the same time.

coun try /kun ′ trē/ *n., pl.* **coun tries. 1.** any area of land; region. **2.** the people of a nation.

cou sin /kuz ′ in/ *n.* the son or daughter of an aunt or uncle.

cray on /krā ′ on, krā ′ ən/ *n.* a colored stick made of a waxed material used for drawing or writing. —*v.* to use crayons to draw or color.

cre a tion /krē ā ′ shən/ *n.* **1.** the act of causing something to exist or happen. **2.** the world and all the things in it.

crea ture /krē ′ chər/ *n.* a living person or animal.

crev ice /krev ′ is/ *n.* a narrow crack into or through something.

crew /krü/ *n.* a group of people who work together.

crim son /krim ′ zən/ *n.* a deep red color. —*adj.* having the color crimson.

crutch /kruch/ *n., pl.* **crutch es.** a support that helps a lame person in walking.

cus tom /kus ′ təm/ *n.* **1.** a way of acting that has become accepted by many people. **2. customs.** taxes that a government collects on products that are brought in from a foreign country —*adj.* made the way the buyer wants or needs.

cym bals /sim ′ bəls/ *n.* a pair of circular metal plates that produce a ringing sound when clashed together.

...D.........

dair y /dâr ′ ē/ *n.* **dair ies.** a place where milk and cream are stored or made into butter and cheese.

dance /dans/ *v.* **danced, danc ing.** *v.* to move the body or feet in time to music. —*n.* a particular set of steps or movements done in time to music.

dar ing /dâr ′ ing/ *n.* courage or boldness; bravery. —*adj.* courageous and bold; brave; fearless.

Dec. an abbreviation for *December*.

dec i mal /des ′ ə məl/ *adj.* based on the number 10. In the United States, money is based on the decimal system. —*n.* a fraction with denominator of 10, or a multiple of 10.

de clare /di klâr ′/ *v.* **de clared, de clar ing. 1.** to announce or make something known. **2.** to say strongly and firmly.

deer /dîr/ *n., pl.* **deer.** an animal that has hooves, chews its cud, and runs very fast.

de par ture /di pär ′ chər/ *n.* the act of leaving.

de spair /di spâr ′/ *n.* a complete loss of hope. —*v.* to give up or lose hope.

/a/	at
/ā/	ape
/ä/	far
/â/	care
/e/	end
/ē/	me
/i/	it
/ī/	ice
/î/	pierce
/o/	hot
/ō/	old
/ô/	song
/ôr/	fork
/oi/	oil
/ou/	out
/u/	up
/ū/	use
/ü/	rule
/ u̇/	pull
/ûr/	turn
/ch/	chin
/ng/	sing
/sh/	shop
/th/	thin
/th/	this
/hw/	white
/zh/	treasure
/ə/	about
	taken
	pencil
	lemon
	circus

adj.	adjective
adv.	adverb
conj.	conjunction
contr.	contraction
def.	definition
interj.	interjection
n.	noun
pl.	plural
prep.	preposition
pron.	pronoun
sing.	singular
v.	verb
v.i.	intransitive verb
v.t.	transitive verb

de stroy /di stroi ′/ *v.* to ruin completely; wreck.

de vice /di vīs ′/ *n.* **1.** something made for a particular purpose. **2.** a plan or scheme.

did n't /did ′ ənt/ *contr.* shortened form of "did not."

dig it /dij ′ it/ *n.* **1.** one of the numerals 0, 1, 2, 3, 4, 5, 6, 7, 8, or 9. **2.** a finger, toe, or claw.

di rec tion /di rek ′ shən, dī rek ′ shən/ *n.* **1.** management or control, guidance. **2.** the line or course along which something moves, faces, or lies.

dirt y /dûr ′ tē/ *adj.* **dirt i er, dirt i est. 1.** soiled; not clean. **2.** angry or resentful.

dis- a prefix that means not or opposite. *Disapprove* means not to approve.

dis tance /dis ′ təns/ *n.* **1.** the amount of space between two points. **2.** a point that is far away.

ditch /dich/ *n., pl.* **ditch es.** a long, narrow hole dug in the ground.

dive /dīv/ *v.* **dived** or **dove, dived, div ing. 1.** to plunge headfirst into water. **2.** to go, move, or drop suddenly and quickly. —*n.* a headfirst plunge into water. **2.** a quick, steep plunge.

dol lar /dol ′ ər/ *n.* a unit of money in the United States and Canada.

do mi no /dom ′ ə nō ′/ *n., pl.* **dom i noes.** a small black tile divided into halves, each half being blank or having from one to six black dots, used in playing certain games.

do mi noes /dom ′ ə nōs ′/ *pl. n.* **1.** a game played with small black tiles marked with dots. **2.** plural of *domino.*

done /dun/ *v.* past participle of do. —*adj.* cooked.

don key /dong ′ kē, dung ′ kē/ *n.* a tame ass.

don't /dōnt/ *contr.* shortened form of "do not."

Dr. an abbreviation for *doctor.*

dra gon /drag ′ ən/ *n.* an imaginary beast that is supposed to look like a giant lizard with claws and wings.

drag on fly /drag ′ ən flī ′/ *n., pl.* **drag on flies.** an insect that has a long, thin body and two pairs of wings.

draw /drô/ *v.* **drew, drawn, draw ing. 1.** to move. **2.** to take out; bring out. **3.** to make a mark or picture with lines,

114

using a writing tool. **4.** to bring forth. **5.** to close; shut. **6.** to take in by inhaling —*n.* **1.** the act of drawing. **2.** a game or contest that ends with an even score or no winner; tie.

drew /drü/ *v.* the past tense of *draw*.

dry /drī/ *adj.* **dri er, dri est. 1.** not wet or damp. **2.** not in or under water. **3.** thirsty. **4.** not interesting; dull. —*v.* **dried, dry ing.** to make or become dry.

due /dü, dū/ *n.* something that is owed. —*adj.* **1.** owed or owing. **2.** expected or supposed to arrive or be ready. **due to.** because of.

dy na mite /dī ′ nə mīt ′/ *n.* a substance that explodes with great force. Dynamite is used to blow up old buildings and blast openings in rocks. —*v.* **dy na mit ed, dy na mit ing.** to blow something up with dynamite.

··· E ···············

ea gle /ē ′ gəl/ *n.* any of several large birds that hunt and feed on small animals and fish.

ear ly /ûr ′ lē/ *adj.* **earl i er,**

earl i est. 1. in or near the beginning. **2.** before the usual time. —*adv.* **1.** in or near the beginning. **2.** before the customary or expected time. *I arrived at work early.*

ear nest /ûr ′ nist/ *adj.* sincere about something.

east /ēst/ *n.* the direction where the sun rises. —*adj.* **1.** toward or in the east. **2.** coming from the east. —*adv.* toward the east.

eas y /ē ′ zē/ *adj.* **eas i er, eas i est. 1.** not hard to do. **2.** not strict or difficult.

eight /āt/ *n.* one more than seven.

eight een /ā ′ tēn ′/ *n., adj.* eight more than ten; 18.

eighth /āth/ *adj., n.* next after the seventh. —*n.* one of eight equal parts; 1/8.

eight y /ā ′ tē/ *n., pl.* **eight ies.** *adj.* eight times ten; 80.

el bow /el ′ bō/ *n.* **1.** the joint between the upper arm and the lower arm. **2.** something having the same shape as a bent elbow. In plumbing, a pipe that curves at a sharp angle is called an elbow. —*v.* to push with the elbows; shove.

em ploy /em ploi ′/ *v.* **1.** to pay someone to do work. **2.** to use.

/a/	at
/ā/	ape
/ä/	far
/â/	care
/e/	end
/ē/	me
/i/	it
/ī/	ice
/î/	pierce
/o/	hot
/ō/	old
/ô/	song
/ôr/	fork
/oi/	oil
/ou/	out
/u/	up
/ū/	use
/ü/	rule
/ù/	pull
/ûr/	turn
/ch/	chin
/ng/	sing
/sh/	shop
/th/	thin
/th/	this
/hw/	white
/zh/	treasure
/ə/	about
	taken
	pencil
	lemon
	circus

adj.	adjective
adv.	adverb
conj.	conjunction
contr.	contraction
def.	definition
interj.	interjection
n.	noun
pl.	plural
prep.	preposition
pron.	pronoun
sing.	singular
v.	verb
v.i.	intransitive verb
v.t.	transitive verb

emp ty /emp ′ tē/ *adj.*
emp ti er, emp ti est. having nothing in it. —*v.* **emp tied, emp ty ing.** to remove all that is in something.

end less /end ′ lis/ *adj.* without end; going on forever. —**end less ly,** *adv.* —**end less ness,** *n.*

en joy ment /en joi ′ mənt/ *n.* pleasure; joy.

-er a suffix that means a person or thing that does something. A *teacher* is a person who teaches.

e rase /i rās ′/ *v.* **e rased, e ras ing. 1.** to remove by rubbing, scratching, or wiping off. **2.** to remove recording from.

e ven /ē ′ vən/ *adj.* **1.** free from changes; regular. **2.** at the same height. **3.** completely flat. **4.** the same or equal. **5.** able to be divided by 2 without leaving a remainder. —*adv.* **1.** as a matter of fact; actually. **2.** still; yet. **3.** at the same moment. —*v.* to make or become even.

eve ry bod y /ev ′ rē bod ′ ē/ *pron.* every person.

ex- a prefix that means former or earlier. This prefix is followed by a hyphen. *Ex-president* means former president.

ex er cise /ek ′ sər sīz ′/ *n.* **1.** activity that trains or improves the body or the mind. **2.** use or practice. **3.** a ceremony or program. —*v.* **ex er cised,**

ex er cis ing. 1. to put or go through exercises. **2.** to make use of.

... F .... **.......**

face /fās/ *n.* **1.** the front of the head. **2.** the front, main, or outward part of something. —*v.* **faced, fac ing. 1.** to turn the face toward. **2.** to deal with. *You must face your problem.*

fail ure /fāl ′ yər/ *n.* the act of not succeeding in doing or getting something.

farm er /fär ′ mər/ *n.* a person who owns or works on a farm.

fau cet /fô ′ sit/ *n.* a device for turning on and off the flow of water or another liquid from a pipe, sink, or container.

fear ful /fir ′ fəl/ *adj.* **1.** feeling or showing fear, afraid. —**fear ful ly,** *adv.* —**fear ful ness,** *n.*

fea ture /fē ′ chər/ *n.* **1.** a part or quality of something. **2.** a part of the face. **3.** a motion picture of standard length. **4.** a story of special interest in a magazine or newspaper. —*v.* **fea tured, fea tur ing.** to have as a main attraction.

Feb. an abbreviation for February.

fe male /fē ′ māl/ *adj.* having to do with women or girls; feminine. —*n.* a female person or animal.

few /fū/ *n.* a small number of persons or things. —*adj.* not many.

field /fēld/ *n.* **1.** a piece of open or cleared land. **2.** land that contains or gives a natural resource. **3.** an area of interest or activity. —*v.* to catch, stop, or pick up a ball that has been hit in baseball.

fif teen /fif ′ tēn ′/ *n., adj.* five more than ten; 15.

fifth /fifth/ *adj., n.* next after the fourth. —*n.* one of five equal parts; 1/5.

fif ty /fif ′ tē/ *n., pl.* **fif ties.** *adj.* five times ten; 50. —**fif ti eth,** *adj.*

find /fīnd/ *n.* something that is found. —*v.* **found. 1.** to discover or come upon by accident. **2.** to get or learn by thinking or calculating.

fin ish /fin ′ ish/ *v.* **1.** to bring to an end; complete. **2.** to use up completely. **3.** to treat the surface of in some way. —*n.* **1.** the end of something. **2.** the surface of something.

flash /flash/ *n., pl.* **flash es. 1.** a sudden, short burst of light or flame. **2.** a very short period of time. —*v.* **1.** to be suddenly bright. **2.** to come or move suddenly.

flight /flīt/ *n.* **1.** the distance or course traveled by a bird or aircraft. **2.** a set of stairs or steps between floors or landings of a building. **3.** the act of running away.

flip /flip/ *v.* **flipped, flip ping.** to toss or turn over with a quick, jerking motion.

flour /flour/ *n.* a fine powder that is made by grinding and sifting wheat, rye, or other grains.

flow /flō/ *n.* a long series of things coming steadily; stream. —*v.* **1.** to move along steadily in a stream. **2.** to hang or fall loosely.

flow er /flou ′ ər/ *n.* **1.** the part of a plant that makes seeds; blossom. **2.** a plant grown for its showy petals. —*v.* to produce flowers; blossom.

flute /flūt/ *n.* a long thin musical instrument that is played by blowing across a hole at one end.

fog gy /fôg ′ ē, fog ′ ē/ *adj.* **fog gi er, fog gi est. 1.** full of or hidden by fog. **2.** confused or unclear.

forth /fôrth/ *adv.* **1.** forward. **2.** out into view.

for ty /fôr ′ tē/ *n., pl.* **for ties.** *adj.* four times ten; 40. —**for ti eth,** *adj.*

/a/	at
/ā/	ape
/ä/	far
/â/	care
/e/	end
/ē/	me
/i/	it
/ī/	ice
/î/	pierce
/o/	hot
/ō/	old
/ô/	song
/ôr/	fork
/oi/	oil
/ou/	out
/u/	up
/ū/	use
/ü/	rule
/u̇/	pull
/ûr/	turn
/ch/	chin
/ng/	sing
/sh/	shop
/th/	thin
/th/	this
/hw/	white
/zh/	treasure
/ə/	about
	taken
	pencil
	lemon
	circus

adj.	adjective
adv.	adverb
conj.	conjunction
contr.	contraction
def.	definition
interj.	interjection
n.	noun
pl.	plural
prep.	preposition
pron.	pronoun
sing.	singular
v.	verb
v.i.	intransitive verb
v.t.	transitive verb

foul /foul/ *adj.* **1.** very unpleasant or dirty. **2.** cloudy, rainy, or stormy. **3.** very bad; evil. **4.** breaking the rules; unfair. **5.** outside the foul line in a baseball game. —*n.* **1.** a breaking of rules. **2.** a baseball that is hit outside the foul line.—*v.* **1.** to make dirty. **2.** to tangle or become tangled. **3.** to hit a foul ball in baseball.

found /found/ *v.* past tense and past participle of *find*.

four teen /fôr ' tēn '/ *n., adj.* four more than ten; 14.

fourth /fôrth/ *adj., n.* next after the third. —*n.* one of four equal parts; 1/4.

fowl /foul/ *n., pl.* **fowl** or **fowls.** one of a number of birds that are used for food.

fox /foks/ *n., pl.* **fox es. 1.** a wild animal which is related to the dog. **2.** a sly or cunning person.

fran tic /fran ' tik/ *adj.* wildly excited by worry or fear.

free /frē/ *adj.* **fre er, fre est. 1.** not under another's control. **2.** not held back or confined. **3.** not troubled or affected by something. **4.** not obstructed. **5.** without cost. —*adv.* without cost. —*v.* **freed, free ing.** to make or set free.

freight /frāt/ *n.* **1.** the carrying of goods by land, air, or water. **2.** the goods carried in this way. —*adj.* cargo.

Fri. an abbreviation for *Friday*.

friend /frend/ *n.* **1.** a person whom one knows well and likes. **2.** a person who supports something.

fright en /frī ' tən/ *v.* to make or become suddenly afraid or alarmed.

frisk y /fris ' kē/ *adj.* **frisk i er, frisk i est.** playful, lively.

front /frunt/ *n.* **1.** the part that faces forward or comes first. **2.** the land that lies along a street or body of water. **3.** a place where fighting is going on between enemy forces. **4.** the boundary line between two air masses of different temperatures. —*adj.* on or near the front. —*v.* to face.

fruit /früt/ *n.* a plant part that contains seeds and is fleshy or juicy and good to eat.

-ful a suffix that means having the qualities of; full of. *Fearful* means full of fear.

fur ni ture /fûr ' ni chər/ *n.* movable articles used in a home or office.

fur ther /fûr ' thər/ *adj.* a comparative of far. —*adv.* more distant in time, space, or degree. —*v.* to help forward; support.

...G.........G....

gal ler y /gal ′ ə rē/ *n., pl.*
gal ler ies. 1. a balcony in a theater or large hall. **2.** a room or building where works of art are shown or sold.

gar den /gär dən/ *n.* a piece of ground where flowers and vegetables are grown. —*v.* to work in a garden.

geese /gēs/ *pl. n.* plural of goose.

gem /jem/ *n.* **1.** a precious gem that has been cut and polished; jewel. **2.** a person or thing that has been thought of as perfect or valuable.

gen er al /jen ′ ər əl/ *n.* **1.** for all; for the whole. **2.** an armed forces officer of the highest rank.

gen ius /jēn yəs/ *n., pl.*
gen ius es. great ability to think or to invent or create things.

gen tle /jen ′ təl/ *adj.* **gen tler, gen tlest. 1.** mild and kindly. **2.** easy to handle; tame. **3.** not steep.

gen u ine /jen ′ ū in/ *adj.*
1. real. **2.** sincere, honest.

ge og ra phy /jē og ′ rə fē/ *n., pl.* **ge og ra phies 1.** the science that deals with the surface of the earth and the plant, animal, and human life on it. **2.** the surface or natural features of a place or region.

ger bil /jûr ′ bəl/ *n.* a small rodent that is native to deserts in Africa and Asia.

germ /jûrm/ *n.* a tiny particle that can cause disease. Viruses and bacteria are germs.

gi ant /jī ′ ənt/ *n.* a person or thing that is very large, powerful, or important. —*adj.* very large.

gi raffe /jə raf ′/ *n.* a large animal that lives in Africa. It has a very long neck, long, thin legs, and a coat with brown patches.

gla cier /glā ′ shər/ *n.* a large mass of ice in very cold regions or on the tops of high mountains. A glacier is formed by snow that does not melt.

glare /glâr/ *n.* **1.** a strong, unpleasant light. **2.** an angry look or stare. —*v.* **glared, glar ing. 1.** to shine with a strong, unpleasant light. **2.** to give an angry look.

gloom y /glü ′ mē/ *adj.*
gloom i er, gloom i est.
1. sad. **2.** dim.

goal /gōl/ *n.* **1.** something that a person wants and tries to get or become; aim; purpose. **2.** a place in certain games where players must get the ball or puck in order to score. **3.** the point or

/a/	at
/ā/	ape
/ä/	far
/â/	care
/e/	end
/ē/	me
/i/	it
/ī/	ice
/i/	pierce
/o/	hot
/ō/	old
/ô/	song
/ôr/	fork
/oi/	oil
/ou/	out
/u/	up
/ū/	use
/ü/	rule
/u̇/	pull
/ûr/	turn
/ch/	chin
/ng/	sing
/sh/	shop
/th/	thin
/th/	this
/hw/	white
/zh/	treasure
/ə/	about
	taken
	pencil
	lemon
	circus

adj.	adjective
adv.	adverb
conj.	conjunction
contr.	contraction
def.	definition
interj.	interjection
n.	noun
pl.	plural
prep.	preposition
pron.	pronoun
sing.	singular
v.	verb
v.i.	intransitive verb
v.t.	transitive verb

points made by getting the ball or puck into such a place.

go ing /gō ′ ing/ *v.* moving from one place to another.

goose /güs/ *n., pl.* **geese. 1.** a bird that looks like a duck but is larger and has a longer neck. **2.** a female bird. A male goose is called a gander.

grain /grān/ *n.* **1.** the seed of wheat, corn, and other cereal plants. **2.** a tiny, hard piece of something. **3.** the lines and other marks that run through wood, stone, and other things.

grease /grēs, grēz/ *n.* **1.** melted animal fat. **2.** a very thick, oily material. —*v.* to rub or put grease on or in.

groan /grōn/ *n.* a deep sad sound —*v.* to make a deep, sad sound.

ground /ground/ *n.* the part of the earth that is solid; soil; land. —*v.* to force to stay on the ground or to come down to the ground.

group /grüp/ *n.* a number of persons or things together. —*v.* to form or put into a group or groups.

grove /grōv/ *n.* a group of trees standing together.

grow /grō/ *v.* **grew, grown, grow ing. 1.** to become bigger; increase. **2.** to become.

guess /ges/ *v.* to form an opinion without having enough knowledge or facts to be sure. —*n.* an opinion formed without having enough knowledge or facts to be sure.

H

hair less /hâr ′ lis/ *adj.* without hair.

half /haf/ *n., pl.* **halves.** one of two equal parts. —*adj.* being one of two equal parts. —*adv.* partly; somewhat.

hap pen /hap ′ ən/ *v.* **1.** to take place; occur. **2.** to take place without plan or reason. **3.** to come or go by chance. **4.** to be done.

hard ly /härd ′ lē/ *adv.* **1.** just about; barely. **2.** not likely; surely not.

harm ful /härm ′ fəl/ *adj.* causing harm; damaging. —**harm ful ly,** *adv.* —**harm ful ness,** *n.*

have n't /hav ′ ənt/ *contr.* shortened form of "have not."

health y /hel ′ thē/ *adj.* **health i er, health i est.** having, showing, or giving good health.

hear /hîr/ *v.* **heard** /hurd/,

hear ing. 1. to receive sound through the ears. **2.** to listen to. **3.** to get information about.

heart /härt/ *n.* the hollow organ in the body that pumps blood through the arteries and veins.

heav y /hev ′ ē/ *adj.* **heav i er, heav i est. 1.** having great weight. **2.** large in size or amount. **3.** hard to do, carry out, or bear.

hedge /hej/ *n.* a row of shrubs or small trees planted together. —*v.* **hedged, hedg ing. 1.** to surround, close in, or separate with a hedge. **2.** to avoid answering a question directly.

height /hīt/ *n.* **1.** the distance from bottom to top. **2.** the highest point.

help less /help ′ lis/ *adj.* not able to take care of oneself. **—help less ly,** *adv.* **—help less ness,** *n.*

he ro ic /hi rō ′ ik/ *adj.* **1.** very brave; courageous. **2.** describing the deeds of heroes.

high /hī/ *adj.* **1.** tall. **2.** greater than others. —*adv.* at or to a high place. —*n.* **1.** a high place or point. **2.** the arrangement of gears in an automobile, bicycle, or other vehicle that gives the greatest speed.

hinge /hinj/ *n.* a joint on which a door or a gate moves back and forth or up and down.

hob by /hob ′ ē/ *n., pl.* **hob bies.** an activity done regularly in one's spare time for pleasure.

hock ey /hok ′ ē/ *n.* a game played on ice or on a field. Each team uses curved sticks and tries to get the puck into the other team's goal.

hole /hōl/ *n.* **1.** hollow place. **2.** the burrow of an animal.

hol low /hol ′ ō/ *n.* a hole or empty space. —*v.* to make by digging out. —*adj.* **1.** curved in like a cup or bowl; sunken. **2.** deep and echoing. **3.** not solid.

home less /hōm ′ lis/ *adj.* having no home.

hope ful /hōp ′ fəl/ *adj.* having or showing hope. **—hope ful ly,** *adv.* **—hope ful ness,** *n.*

ho ri zon /hə rī ′ zən/ *n.* the line where the sky and the ground or the sea seem to meet.

horse back /hôrs ′ bak ′/ *n.* the back of a horse. —*adv.* on the back of a horse.

huge /hūj/ *adj.* **hug er, hug est.** great in size or amount.

hun dred /hun ′ drid/ *n., adj.* ten times ten; 100.

hun gry /hung ′ grē/ *adj.* **hun gri er, hun gri est. 1.** desiring or needing food. **2.** having a strong desire or craving.

/a/	at
/ā/	ape
/ä/	far
/â/	care
/e/	end
/ē/	me
/i/	it
/ī/	ice
/î/	pierce
/o/	hot
/ō/	old
/ô/	song
/ôr/	fork
/oi/	oil
/ou/	out
/u/	up
/ū/	use
/ü/	rule
/ù/	pull
/ûr/	turn
/ch/	chin
/ng/	sing
/sh/	shop
/th/	thin
/th/	this
/hw/	white
/zh/	treasure
/ə/	about
	taken
	pencil
	lemon
	circus

adj.	adjective
adv.	adverb
conj.	conjunction
contr.	contraction
def.	definition
interj.	interjection
n.	noun
pl.	plural
prep.	preposition
pron.	pronoun
sing.	singular
v.	verb
v.i.	intransitive verb
v.t.	transitive verb

hur ry /hûr ′ ē, hur ′ ē/ *v.* **hur ried, hur ry ing.** to move or act with speed. —*n.* the act of hurrying.

hurt /hûrt/ *v.* **hurt, hurt ing. 1.** to cause pain or injury. **2.** to be painful. —*n.* a pain or injury.

hutch /huch/ *n., pl.* **hutch es.** a house for rabbits or other small animals.

hy drant /hī ′ drənt/ *n.* a wide, covered pipe that sticks out of the ground and is attached underground to a water supply. Firefighters attach hoses to hydrants to get water to put out fires.

ice berg /īs ′ bûrg ′/ *n.* a very large piece of floating ice that has broken off from a glacier. Most of an iceberg is underwater.

i ci cle /ī ′ si kəl/ *n.* a pointed, hanging piece of ice. It is formed by water that freezes as it drips.

i dle /ī ′ dəl/ *adj.* **1.** lazy. **2.** not busy. —*v.* **1.** to spend time doing nothing. **2.** to run slowly and out of gear.

inch /inch/ *n., pl.* **inch es. 1.** a measure of length that equals 1/12 of a foot, or 2.54 centimeters. **2.** the smallest distance, amount, or degree. —*v.* to move very slowly.

in stance /in ′ stəns/ *n.* an example; case.

is land /ī ′ lənd/ *n.* a body of land completely surrounded by water.

is sue /ish ′ ü/ *n.* **1.** the act of sending or giving out. **2.** a subject that is being discussed. —*v.* **is sued, is su ing.** to send or give out.

it's /its/ *contr.* shortened form of "it is" and "it has."

jack et /jak ′ it/ *n.* **1.** a short coat. **2.** an outer covering for a record or book.

Jan. an abbreviation for *January.*

jock ey /jok ′ ē/ *n.* a person who rides horses in races.

jog /jog/ *v.* **jogged, jog ging.** to run or move at a slow, steady pace.

joint /joint/ *n.* the place or part where two or more bones meet or come together. —*adj.* belonging to or done by two or more people.

joy ful /joi ′ fəl/ *adj.* feeling, showing, or causing great happiness; glad. **—joy ful ly,** *adv.* **—joy ful ness,** *n.*

juice /jüs/ *n.* **1.** the liquid from vegetables, fruits, or meats. **2.** a fluid produced inside the body.

... K ...

kitch en /kich ′ ən/ *n.* a room or place where food is cooked.

kit ten /kit ′ ən/ *n.* a young cat.

knife /nīf/ *n., pl.* **knives.** a tool used for cutting. *—v.* **knifed, knif ing.** to cut or stab with a knife.

know /nō/ *v.* **knew, known, know ing. 1.** to understand clearly. **2.** to be acquainted or familiar with. **3.** to have skill or experience with.

... L ...

land scap er /land ′ skāp ər/ *n.* a person who improves an area by planting trees and other plants.

large /lärj/ *adj.* **larg er, larg est.** big in size or amount.

lar i at /lar ′ ē ət, lâr ′ ē ət/ *n.* a long rope with a loop at one end; lasso.

leaf /lēf/ *n., pl.* **leaves. 1.** one of the flat, green parts growing from a stem of a plant. **2.** a sheet of paper. **3.** a movable flat part of the top of a table. *—v.* **1.** to grow leaves. **2.** to turn pages and glance at them quickly.

learn /lûrn/ *v.* **learned** or **learnt, learn ing. 1.** to get to know through study or practice. **2.** to memorize. **3.** to get information about.

least /lēst/ *n.* the smallest thing or amount. *—adj.* smallest; littlest. *—adv.* in the smallest degree. *This year's crop is the least abundant in years.*

lec ture /lek ′ chər/ *n.* **1.** a talk given to an audience. **2.** a scolding. *—v.* **lec tured, lec tur ing. 1.** to give a lecture. **2.** to scold.

-less a suffix that means having no; without. *Hopeless* means having no hope.

les son /les ′ ən/ *n.* **1.** something to be learned. **2.** a period of time given to instruction.

li brar y /lī ′ brer ′ ē, lī ′ brâr ′ ē/ *n.* **li brar ies. 1.** a collection of books, magazines, and newspapers. **2.** a room or building for such a collection.

/a/	at
/ā/	ape
/ä/	far
/â/	care
/e/	end
/ē/	me
/i/	it
/ī/	ice
/î/	pierce
/o/	hot
/ō/	old
/ô/	song
/ôr/	fork
/oi/	oil
/ou/	out
/u/	up
/ū/	use
/ü/	rule
/ù/	pull
/ûr/	turn
/ch/	chin
/ng/	sing
/sh/	shop
/th/	thin
/<u>th</u>/	this
/hw/	white
/zh/	treasure
/ə/	about
	taken
	pencil
	lemon
	circus

adj.	adjective
adv.	adverb
conj.	conjunction
contr.	contraction
def.	definition
interj.	interjection
n.	noun
pl.	plural
prep.	preposition
pron.	pronoun
sing.	singular
v.	verb
v.i.	intransitive verb
v.t.	transitive verb

light house /līt ′ hous ′/ *n.* a tower with a strong light on top. It is built near a dangerous place in the water to warn or guide ships.

loaf [1] /lōf/ *n., pl.* **loaves.** bread baked in one piece.

loaf [2] /lōf/ *v.* to spend time doing little or nothing.

lo ca tion /lō kā ′ shən/ *n.* the place where something is located.

loud /loud/ *adj.* **1.** having a strong sound; not quiet. **2.** too bright; gaudy. —*adv.* in a loud manner. —**loud ly,** *adv.* —**loud ness,** *n.*

loy al /loi ′ əl/ *adj.* having or showing strong or lasting affection and support.

luck y /luk ′ ē/ *adj.* **1.** having or bringing good luck. **2.** caused by good luck.

ma chine /mə shēn ′/ *n.* a device that does some particular job.

mag ic /maj ′ ik/ *n.* the art or skill of doing tricks to entertain people. —*adj.* using magic.

mail /māl/ *n.* **1.** letters, cards, and packages that are sent or received through a post office. **2.** the system by which mail is sent, moved, or delivered. —*v.* to send by mail.

make /māk/ *v.* **made, mak ing. 1.** to cause to be or happen. **2.** to add up; amount to. **3.** to earn. —*n.* the style or type of something that is made and sold; brand.

male /māl/ *adj.* of or having to do with men or boys. *A male deer is called a buck.* —*n.* a male person, animal, or plant.

Mar. an abbreviation for *March.*

marsh /märsh/ *n., pl.* **marsh es.** low wet lands.

match [1] /mach/ *n., pl.* **match es. 1.** a person or thing suitable with another. **2.** a game or contest. —*v.* to be like something.

match [2] /mach/ *n., pl.* **match es.** a short thin piece of wood or cardboard used to start a fire.

mea sles /mē ′ zəlz/ *n.* a disease that causes a rash of small red spots, a fever, and the symptoms of a bad cold. It is caused by a virus. The word "measles" is used with a singular or plural verb.

men tion /men ′ shən/ *v.* to speak about or refer to. —*n.* a short remark or statement.

mid night /mid ′ nīt ′/ *n.* twelve o'clock at night; the middle of the night.

might y /mī ′ tē/ *adj.* **might i er, might i est.** great in power, size, or amount.

mild /mīld/ *adj.* gentle or calm; not harsh or sharp.

mile /mīl/ *n.* a measure of distance equal to 5,280 feet.

mil lion /mil ′ yən/ *n., adj.* one thousand times one thousand; 1,000,000.

min er /mī ′ nər/ *n.* a person who mines, especially a person whose occupation is digging in the earth for coal, mineral oils, or other materials.

mi nor /mī nər/ *adj.* small in importance or size. —*n.* a person who is not old enough to vote or be legally responsible for his or her own affairs.

mix /miks/ *v.* to blend, combine, or join. —*n.* something that is made by mixing.

moist /moist/ *adj.* slightly wet; damp.

mois ture /mois ′ chər/ *n.* water or other liquid in the air or on a surface.

Mon. an abbreviation for *Monday.*

mon key /mung ′ kē/ *n.* any of a group of intelligent, furry animals with long tails and hands

and feet that can grasp things.

moth /môth/ *n.* an insect that looks like a butterfly. Moths have thick bodies and fly mostly at night.

mo tion /mō ′ shən/ *n.* **1.** the act of changing place or position. **2.** a formal suggestion made at a meeting. —*v.* to move the hand or another part of the body as a sign of something.

mouth /mouth, mou<u>th</u>/ *n.* **1.** the opening through which people and animals take in food. **2.** any opening that is like a mouth. *the mouth of a river.* —*v.* to say or repeat in an insincere way.

move /müv/ *n.* an action planned to bring about a result. —*v.* **moved, mov ing.** to go forward; advance.

nap /nap/ *v.* **napped, nap ping. 1.** to sleep for a short while. **2.** to be unprepared.

nar rate /nar ′ āt, na rāt ′, nâr ′ āt/ *v.* **nar rat ed, nar rat ing.** to tell or relate.

nar row /nar ′ ō/ *n.* the narrow part of a body of water. —*v.* to make or become narrow. —*adj.*

/a/ at
/ā/ ape
/ä/ far
/â/ care
/e/ end
/ē/ me
/i/ it
/ī/ ice
/î/ pierce
/o/ hot
/ō/ old
/ô/ song
/ôr/ fork
/oi/ oil
/ou/ out
/u/ up
/ū/ use
/ü/ rule
/ù/ pull
/ûr/ turn
/ch/ chin
/ng/ sing
/sh/ shop
/th/ thin
/<u>th</u>/ this
/hw/ white
/zh/ treasure
/ə/ about
taken
pencil
lemon
circus

125

adj.	adjective
adv.	adverb
conj.	conjunction
contr.	contraction
def.	definition
interj.	interjection
n.	noun
pl.	plural
prep.	preposition
pron.	pronoun
sing.	singular
v.	verb
v.i.	intransitive verb
v.t.	transitive verb

1. not wide or broad. **2.** barely successful; close.

na tion /nā ′ shən/ *n.* **1.** a group of people living in a particular area under one government. **2.** a particular land where people live; country.

na ture /nā ′ chər/ *n.* **1.** the basic character of a person or thing. **2.** the physical universe. **3.** sort or kind. —**nat u ral,** *adj.*

neat /nēt/ *adj.* **1.** clean and orderly; tidy. **2.** having or showing care for keeping things in order. **3.** done in a clever way. **4.** wonderful or fine.

neigh bor /nā ′ bər/ *n.* a person who lives in a house or apartment next to or near.

nice /nīs/ *adj.* pleasant or agreeable.

nick el /nik ′ əl/ *n.* a hard, silver-colored metal.

niece /nēs/ *n.* **1.** the daughter of one's brother or sister. **2.** the daughter of one's brother-in-law or sister-in-law.

nine /nīn/ *n., adj.* one more than eight; 9.

nine teen /nīn ′ tēn ′/ *n., adj.* nine more than ten; 19.

nine ty /nīn ′ tē/ *n., pl.* **nine ties.** *adj.* nine times ten; 90.

nois y /noi ′ zē/ *adj.* **nois i er,**

nois i est. making much noise.

no tice /nō ′ tis/ *n.* **1.** the condition of being seen or observed. **2.** a warning or announcement.

Nov. an abbreviation for *November*.

nu mer al /nü ′ mər əl, nū ′ mər əl/ *n.* a figure or figures which stand for a number.

nurse /nûrs/ *n.* a person who is trained to help sick people. —*v.* **nursed, nurs ing. 1.** to take care of. **2.** to be fed from a nipple.

o bey /ō bā ′/ *v.* to carry out or follow orders or laws.

o cean /ō ′ shən/ *n.* the whole body of salt water that covers nearly three fourths of the earth's surface.

Oct. an abbreviation for *October*.

of fice /ô ′ fis/ *n.* **1.** a place where the work of a business or profession is done. **2.** all the people who work in such a place. **3.** a position of authority.

of ten /ô ′ fən/ *adv.* many times;frequently.

once /wuns/ *adv.* **1.** one time.

2. in a time now past. —*n.* one single time. —*conj.* as soon as; when.

one /wun/ *n.* the first and lowest number; 1. —*adj.* being a particular person, thing, or group. —*pron.* a particular person or thing.

on ly /ōn ′ lē/ *adj.* **1.** alone of its kind; solitary. **2.** best of all. —*adv.* **1.** no more than. **2.** no one or nothing other than. **3.** no time or place except. —*conj.* except that.

o pen /ō ′ pən/ *adj.* **1.** allowing movement in, out, or through. **2.** not closed in or covered; having no barriers. **3.** spread out or unfolded. **4.** free to be used; available. **5.** able or ready to take in new ideas, facts, or beliefs. **6.** honest; frank. **7.** ready to do business. **8.** having spaces, holes, or gaps between the parts. —*v.* **1.** to make or become open. **2.** to have an opening. **3.** to spread out; unfold. **4.** to set up or become available. **5.** to begin; start. —*n.* any space or area that is not closed in or hidden.

o pin ion /ə pin ′ yən/ *n.* **1.** a belief based on what a person thinks. **2.** A formal statement made by an expert. *I wanted to get a lawyer's opinion before I signed the contract.*

-or a suffix that means a person

or thing that does something. *Inventor* means a person who invents.

out side /out ′ sīd ′, out ′ sīd ′, out ′ sīd ′/ *n.* the outer side. —*adj.* on the outside; outer. —*adv.* on or to the outside; outdoors. —*prep.* beyond the limits or range of.

o ver /ō ′ vər/ *prep.* **1.** in a position higher than. **2.** from one side or end to the other. —*adv.* above and beyond the top or edge. —*adj.* at the end.

o ver flow /ō ′ vər flō ′, ō ′ vər flō ′/ *v.* **o ver flown, o ver flow ing. 1.** to flow beyond the usual limits. **2.** to be so full that the contents flow over; to be very full. —*n.* something that overflows.

o ver hear /ō ′ vər hir ′/ *v.* **o ver heard** /ō ′ vər hûrd ′/. to hear something one is not supposed to hear.

ox /oks/ *n., pl.* **ox en.** the adult male of domestic cattle.

ox en /ok ′ sən/ *pl. n.* plural of ox.

oy ster /oi ′ stər/ *n.* an animal that has a soft body and a rough, hinged shell. Oysters are found in shallow waters along coasts.

/a/ at
/ā/ ape
/ä/ far
/â/ care
/e/ end
/ē/ me
/i/ it
/ī/ ice
/î/ pierce
/o/ hot
/ō/ old
/ô/ song
/ôr/ fork
/oi/ oil
/ou/ out
/u/ up
/ū/ use
/ü/ rule
/ù/ pull
/ûr/ turn
/ch/ chin
/ng/ sing
/sh/ shop
/th/ thin
/th/ this
/hw/ white
/zh/ treasure
/ə/ about
taken
pencil
lemon
circus

adj.	adjective
adv.	adverb
conj.	conjunction
contr.	contraction
def.	definition
interj.	interjection
n.	noun
pl.	plural
prep.	preposition
pron.	pronoun
sing.	singular
v.	verb
v.i.	intransitive verb
v.t.	transitive verb

pain ful /pān ′ fəl/ *adj.* causing pain. —**pain ful ly,** *adv.* —**pain ful ness,** *n.*

pain less /pān ′ lis/ *adj.* causing no pain. —**pain less ly,** *adv.* —**pain less ness,** *n.*

pa per /pā ′ pər/ *n.* a material that is used for writing and printing. —*v.* to cover with wallpaper. *The workers papered the hall.*

paste /pāst/ *n.* any soft, smooth, very thick mixture. —*v.* **past ed, past ing. 1.** to stick with paste. **2.** to cover with something stuck on with paste.

patch /pach/ *n., pl.* **patch es. 1.** a small piece of material. **2.** a small area that is different from what is around it. —*v.* to cover or repair with a patch.

patch work /pach ′ wûrk ′/ *n.* pieces of cloth of different colors and shapes that are sewed together.

peace ful /pēs ′ fəl/ *adj.* free from war or disorder; quiet and calm. —**peace ful ly,** *adv.* —**peace ful ness,** *n.*

pearl /pûrl/ *n.* a small, round gem that is white or cream in color and has a soft, glowing shine. Pearls are found inside the shells of certain kinds of oysters.

pen cil /pen ′ səl/ *n.* a long thin tool for writing or drawing. —*v.* to write, draw, or mark with a pencil.

perch [1] /pûrch/ *n., pl.* **perch es. 1.** a bar, branch, or anything else a bird can rest on. **2.** any raised place for sitting or standing. —*v.* to sit or rest on a perch.

perch [2] /purch/ *n., pl.* **perch** or **perch es.** a small fish that is found in fresh water in North America and most parts of Europe.

per fect /pûr ′ fikt, pər fekt ′/ *adj.* **1.** without a mistake or fault. —*v.* to make or complete without any mistakes.

per son /pûr ′ sən/ *n.* **1.** a man, woman, or child. **2.** any of three groups of personal pronouns and verb forms.

pick [1] /pik/ *n.* a pointed tool.

pick [2] /pik/ *v.* **1.** to select or choose. **2.** to cause on purpose. —*n.* **1.** the best one or ones. **2.** a small thin piece of plastic or other material.

pic nic /pik ′ nik/ *n.* a party or

trip for which food is taken along and eaten outside. —*v.* **pic nicked, pic nick ing.** to go on or have a picnic.

pic ture /pik ′ chər/ *n.* **1.** a painting, drawing, or photograph. **2.** a likeness or perfect example. —*v.* **pic tured, pic tur ing.** to draw or paint a picture of.

pi lot /pī ′ lət/ *n.* a person who operates an aircraft, spacecraft, or large ship. —*v.* to act as a pilot.

pinch /pinch/ *n., pl.* **pinch es. 1.** a sharp squeeze. **2.** an amount that can be held between the thumb and a finger. **3.** a time of need or emergency. —*v.* **1.** to squeeze between surfaces. **2.** to make thin or wrinkled.

pipe line /pīp ′ līn ′/ *n.* a line of pipes for carrying a liquid or gas over a long distance.

pi rate /pī ′ rit/ *n.* a person who robs ships at sea.

place /plās/ *n.* **1.** location; area. **2.** a passage in a book. *I lost my place in the book.* —*v.* **placed, plac ing.** to put or be in a particular spot or location.

plas tic /plas ′ tik/ *n.* any of a number of artificially made substances that can be molded and shaped into materials or objects.

—*adj.* made of plastic.

play ful /plā ′ fəl/ *adj.* **1.** wanting or liking to play; lively. **2.** meant to amuse or tease. —**play ful ly,** *adv.* —**play ful ness,** *n.*

play ground /plā ′ ground/ *n.* an outdoor area for children.

please /plēz/ *v.* **pleased, pleas ing. 1.** to give pleasure to. **2.** to want or prefer. **3.** to be so kind as to.

plow /plou/ *n.* a device for clearing away matter in its path. *v.* to move.

plunge /plunj/ *v.* **1.** to put in suddenly. **2.** to dive or fall suddenly.—*n.* the act of plunging.

pock et /pok ′ it/ *n.* a small bag or pouch that is sewn on or into a garment, suitcase, or purse. —*adj.* small enough to be carried in the pocket. —*v.* to put in a pocket.

po et ic /pō et ′ ik/ *adj.* of or like poetry.

poi son /poi ′ zən/ *n.* **1.** a substance that causes serious injury, illness, or death by its chemical action on a living thing. **2.** anything that harms, corrupts, or destroys. —*v.* **1.** to give poison to. **2.** to put poison in. —*adj.* able to poison; poisonous.

/a/	at
/ā/	ape
/ä/	far
/â/	care
/e/	end
/ē/	me
/i/	it
/ī/	ice
/î/	pierce
/o/	hot
/ō/	old
/ô/	song
/ôr/	fork
/oi/	oil
/ou/	out
/u/	up
/ū/	use
/ü/	rule
/ù/	pull
/ûr/	turn
/ch/	chin
/ng/	sing
/sh/	shop
/th/	thin
/<u>th</u>/	this
/hw/	white
/zh/	treasure
/ə/	about
	taken
	pencil
	lemon
	circus

129

adj.   adjective
adv.   adverb
conj.   conjunction
contr.   contraction
def.   definition
interj. interjection
n.   noun
pl.   plural
prep.   preposition
pron.   pronoun
sing.   singular
v.   verb
v.i.   intransitive verb
v.t.   transitive verb

po lice /pə lēs ′/ *n.* a group of persons given power by a government to enforce law and order. "Police" may be used with a singular or plural verb. —*v.* **po liced, po lic ing.** to keep order in.

po ny /pō ′ nē/ *n., pl.* **po nies.** a small kind of horse.

poor /pôr/ *adj.* **1.** having little money. **2.** below standard.

pore [1] /pôr/ *n.* a very small opening in the skin or other surface.

pore [2] /pôr/ *v.* to read or study carefully.

pos ture /pos ′ chər/ *n.* the way a person holds the body when sitting, standing, or walking.

pour /pôr/ *v.* **1.** to flow or cause to flow. **2.** to rain hard.

pow er ful /pou ′ ər fəl/ *adj.* having great power. —**pow er ful ly,** *adv.*

prac ti cal /prak ′ ti kəl/ *adj.* **1.** coming from experience. **2.** having or showing good sense; sensible.

prac tice /prak ′ tis/ *n.* **1.** the doing of some action over and over again to gain skill. **2.** the business of a doctor or other professional. —*v.* **prac ticed,**

prac tic ing. 1. to do some action over and over again to gain a skill. **2.** to work at a profession.

pre pare /pri pâr ′/ *v.* **pre pared, pre par ing.** to make or get ready.

pret ty /prit ′ ē/ *adj.* **pret ti er, pret ti est.** sweetly pleasing; attractive; charming. —*adv.* fairly; quite. *It is raining pretty hard.*

price /prīs/ *n.* **1.** the amount of money for which something is sold or offered for sale. **2.** the cost at which something is gained. —*v.* **priced, pric ing. 1.** to set a price on. **2.** to find out the price of.

prince /prins/ *n.* **1.** a male member of a royal family other than a king. **2.** a nobleman of very high rank.

prin cess /prin ′ sis/ *n., pl.* **prin cess es. 1.** a female member of a royal family other than a king. **2.** a nobleman of very high rank.

prin ci pal /prin ′ sə pəl/ *adj.* greatest or first in importance. —*n.* **1.** the person who is the head of a school. **2.** a person who plays an important role in some activity.

prin ci ple /prin ′ sə pəl/ *n.* a basic truth, law, or belief.

prize [1] /prīz/ *n.* something that is won in a contest or game. —*adj.* that has won or is good enough to win a prize.

prize [2] /prīz/ *v.* **prized, priz ing.** to think very highly of.

prob lem /prob ′ ləm/ *n.* **1.** a question to be thought about and answered. **2.** a condition or fact that causes trouble and must be dealt with.

proof /prüf/ *n.* facts or evidence showing that something is true.

pup py /pup ′ ē/ *n., pl.* **pup pies.** a young dog.

pur ple /pûr pəl/ *n.* the color that is made by mixing red and blue. —*adj.* having the color purple.

pur pose /pûr ′ pəs/ *n.* the reason for which something is made or done.

...R.........R....

rad ish /rad ′ ish/ *n., pl.* **rad ish es.** the small, thick, red or white root of a plant.

rail way /rāl ′ wā ′/ *n.* **1.** a railroad. **2.** the tracks on which a train runs.

rain bow /rān ′ bō ′/ *n.* a curve of colored light seen in the sky. It is caused by the sun's shining through tiny drops of water in the air.

ranch /ranch/ *n., pl.* **ranch es.** a large farm on which large herds of cattle, sheep, and horses are raised. —*v.* to manage or work on a ranch.

range /rānj/ *n.* **1.** the distance or area over which something can extend. **2.** a place set aside for a purpose. **3.** a row or series of mountains. —*v.* **ranged, rang ing.** to extend in some direction.

Rd. an abbreviation for *Road* used in a written address.

re- a prefix that means again. *Reelect* means to elect again.

reach /rēch/ *n., pl.* **reach es.** the distance covered in reaching. —*v.* **1.** to arrive at; come to. **2.** to stretch the arm or hand out.

read /rēd/ *v.* **read** /red/, **read ing. 1.** to look at and understand the meaning of something that is read. **2.** to say aloud something that is written.

re ap pear /rē ′ ə pir ′/ *v.* **re ap peared, re ap pear ing.** to come into sight again; be seen again.

/a/	at
/ā/	ape
/ä/	far
/â/	care
/e/	end
/ē/	me
/i/	it
/ī/	ice
/î/	pierce
/o/	hot
/ō/	old
/ô/	song
/ôr/	fork
/oi/	oil
/ou/	out
/u/	up
/ū/	use
/ü/	rule
/ù/	pull
/ûr/	turn
/ch/	chin
/ng/	sing
/sh/	shop
/th/	thin
/th/	this
/hw/	white
/zh/	treasure
/ə/	about
	taken
	pencil
	lemon
	circus

adj.	adjective
adv.	adverb
conj.	conjunction
contr.	contraction
def.	definition
interj.	interjection
n.	noun
pl.	plural
prep.	preposition
pron.	pronoun
sing.	singular
v.	verb
v.i.	intransitive verb
v.t.	transitive verb

re ar range /rē ′ ə rānj ′/ *v.* **re ar ranged, re ar rang ing.** to arrange again, especially in a different way.

rea son /rē ′ zən/ *n.* **1.** a cause or motive. **2.** a statement that explains something; excuse. —*v.* **1.** to think about clearly. **2.** to try to change a person's mind.

re cess /rē ′ ses, ri ′ ses / *n., pl.* **re cess es. 1.** a time during which work or other activity stops. **2.** a part of a wall that is set back from the rest; niche. **3.** a hidden place or part. —*v.* **re cessed, re cess ing.** to stop work or other activity for a time.

re fin ish /rē fin ′ ish/ *v.* to give a new finish. *refinish the chest.*

re joice /ri jois ′/ *v.* **re joiced, re joic ing.** to show or feel great joy.

re lax /ri laks ′/ *v.* **re lax ing. 1.** to make or become less tense. **2.** to make less strict.

rel ish /rel ′ ish/ *n., pl.* **rel ish es. 1.** a mixture of spices, pickles, chopped vegetables, and other ingredients. **2.** interest or pleasure; enjoyment. —*v.* **2.** to take pleasure in; enjoy.

re move /ri müv ′/ *v.* **re moved, re mov ing. 1.** to take or move away or off. **2.** to do away with; get rid of. **3.** to dis-

miss from an office or position.

re name /rē nām ′/ *v.* **re named, re nam ing.** to name again.

re paint /rē pānt ′/ *v.* to paint again.

re pair /ri pâr ′/ *v.* to put in good condition again; fix; mend. —*n.* the act of repairing.

re place /ri plās ′/ *v.* **re placed, re plac ing. 1.** to take or fill the place of. **2.** to get or give something similar in place of. **3.** to put back.

re run /rē ′ run ′, rē run ′/ *n.* the act of running again. —*v.* **re ran, re run ning.** to show as a rerun.

res cue /res ′ kū/ *v.* **res cued, res cu ing.** to save or free. —*n.* the act of rescuing.

re spect ful /ri spekt ′ fəl/ *adj.* having or showing respect. —**re spect ful ly,** *adv.* —**re spect ful ness,** *n.*

re take /rē tāk ′/ *v.* **re took, re tak ing.** to take again.

re think /rē thingk ′/ *v.* to think about again.

re verse /ri vûrs ′/ *n.* the direct opposite; contrary. —*adj.* opposite in position or direction. —*v.*

re versed, re vers ing. to change to the opposite.

re view /ri vū ′/ *v.* **1.** to study, go over, or examine again. **2.** to give a critical account of. **3.** to make a formal or official inspection of. —*n.* **1.** a studying, going over, or examining again. **2.** a looking back. **3.** an account of a movie, play, book, or other work given to praise or criticize it. **4.** a formal or official inspection.

re wind /rē wīnd ′/ *v.*
re wound, re wind ing. to wind backward to a previous place.

rhyme /rīm/ *n.* **1.** the repetition of similar sound at the end of lines of verse. **2.** a word that sounds like or the same as another. —*v.* **rhymed, rhym ing.** to make a rhyme.

rib bon /rib ′ ən/ *n.* **1.** a band of cloth or other material used for decoration. **2.** a band of material. *a typewriter ribbon.*

ride /rīd/ *v.* **rode, rid den, rid ing. 1.** to sit on a vehicle or animal and make it move in order to be carried by it. **2.** to be carried along. *ride the waves.* —*n.* a short trip on an animal or in a car, train, or other vehicle. **2.** a device on which people ride for amusement.

rock [1] /rok/ *n.* **1.** a piece of stone. **2.** a mass of mineral matter that is formed naturally and is part of the earth's crust.

rock [2] /rok/ *v.* **1.** to move in a gentle way. **2.** to move or shake violently. —*n.* a rocking motion.

rock et /rok ′ it/ *n.* a device that is driven through the air by a stream of hot gases that are released from the rear. —*v.* to move or rise very quickly.

root /rüt, ru̇t/ *n.* **1.** the part of the plant that goes down into the ground. **2.** a part where something begins. —*v.* **1.** to develop roots and begin to grow. **2.** to pull, tear, or get rid of completely.

roy al /roi ′ əl/ *adj.* having to do with a king or queen or their family.

··· **S** ·········· ····

sail /sāl/ *n.* **1.** a large piece of canvas attached to a boat or ship. **2.** a trip or ride in a boat. —*v.* **1.** to move through the water. **2.** to steer or run a boat. **3.** to move smoothly and without difficulty.

sand wich /sand ′ wich, san ′ wich/ *n., pl.* **sand wich es.**

/a/ at
/ā/ ape
/ä/ far
/â/ care
/e/ end
/ē/ me
/i/ it
/ī/ ice
/ î/ pierce
/o/ hot
/ō/ old
/ô/ song
/ôr/ fork
/oi/ oil
/ou/ out
/u/ up
/ū/ use
/ü/ rule
/u̇/ pull
/ûr/ turn
/ch/ chin
/ng/ sing
/sh/ shop
/th/ thin
/th/ this
/hw/ white
/zh/ treasure
/ə/ about
taken
pencil
lemon
circus

two or more slices of bread with a filling between them.

Sat. an abbreviation for *Saturday.*

scale /skāl/ *n.* a device used to find out how heavy something is. —*v.* **scaled, scal ing.** to climb to or over the top of.

scare /skâr/ *v.* **scared, scar ing.** to frighten or become afraid. —*n.* a sudden fear or fright. **—scar y, scar i er, scar i est, scar i ness,** *adj.*

scarf /skärf/ *n., pl.* **scarves** or **scarfs.** a piece of cloth worn about the neck or head.

school [1] /skül/ *n.* **1.** a place for teaching and learning. **2.** the students, teachers, and other people who work at such a place. —*v.* to train or teach.

school [2] /skül/ *n.* a large group of fish or water animals swimming together.

sci ence /sī ′ əns/ *n.* knowledge about things in nature and the universe.

scratch /skrach/ *n., pl.* **scratch es. 1.** a mark made by scraping or cutting. **2.** a harsh, grating sound. —*v.* to scrape or cut with something that is sharp and pointed.

scream /skrēm/ *n.* a loud, shrill, piercing cry or sound. —*v.* to make a loud, shrill, piercing cry or sound.

screech /skrēch/ *v.* to make a shrill, harsh cry or sound. —*n., pl.* **screech es.** a shrill, harsh cry or sound.

screw driv er /skrü ′ drī ′ vər/ *n.* a tool for turning screws.

search /sûrch/ *v.* to examine carefully in order to find something. —*n., pl.* **search es.** the act of searching.

sea weed /sē ′ wēd / *n.* a plant that grows in the sea, especially certain kinds of algae.

sen tence /sen ′ təns/ *n.* **1.** a group of words that gives a complete thought. **2.** a punishment for crime set by a court. —*v.* **sen tenced, sen tenc ing.** to set the punishment of.

Sept. an abbreviation for *September.*

serve /sûrv/ *v.* **served, serv ing. 1.** to set food before. **2.** to be used. *This sofa can serve as a bed.* **3.** to be a servant to. **4.** in some games, to hit the ball before playing. —*n.* in some games the act of hitting a ball in order to begin playing.

sev en teen /sev ′ ən tēn ′/ *n., adj.* seven more than ten; 17.

sha dow /shad ′ ō/ figure made when rays of light are blocked by a person or thing. —*v.* to follow and watch another person closely and secretly.

shape less /shāp ′ lis/ *adj.* without a definite shape. —**shape less ly,** *adv.* **shape less ness,** *n.*

share /shâr/ *n.* one of the equal parts into which the ownership is divided. —*v.* **shared, shar ing.** to use with another.

shelf /shelf/ *n., pl.* **shelves. 1.** a thin piece of wood, metal, or other material fastened to a wall or frame. **2.** anything like a shelf.

shield /shēld/ *n.* **1.** a piece of armor carried on the arm to protect the body or head during battle. **2.** a person or thing that defends or protects. —*v.* to defend or protect.

shirt /shûrt/ *n.* a piece of clothing worn on the upper part of the body.

shoe /shü/ *n.* an outer covering for the foot. —*v.* **shod, shoe ing.** to provide with a shoe or shoes.

show /shō/ *v.* **showed, shown,** or **showed, show ing. 1.** to bring to sight or view; make known. **2.** to point out or lead. —*n.* **1.** something that is seen in public. *a horse show.* **2.** any entertainment in the theater or on radio or television. **3.** a display meant to attract attention. *a show of his knowledge.*

shriek /shrēk/ *n.* a loud, sharp cry or sound. —*v.* to utter a loud, sharp cry or sound.

since /sins/ *adv.* before now. —*prep.* during the time after. —*conj.* during the period after.

six /siks/ *n., pl.* **six es.** *adj.* one more than five.

six teen /siks ′ tēn ′/ *n., adj.* six more than ten; 16.

sketch /skech/ *n., pl.* **sketch es. 1.** a rough quick drawing. **2.** a short piece of writing. —*v.* to make a sketch of.

ski /skē/ *n., pl.* **skis.** one of a pair of long, narrow strips of wood, metal, or plastic that curve upward at the front. —*v.* **ski ing.** to glide on skis.

skill ful /skil ′ fəl/ *adj.* having or showing skill; expert. —**skill ful ly,** *adv.* —**skill ful ness,** *n.*

sleep less /slēp ′ lis/ *adj.* without sleep. —**sleep less ly,** *adv.* —**sleep less ness,** *n.*

/a/	at
/ā/	ape
/ä/	far
/â/	care
/e/	end
/ē/	me
/i/	it
/ī/	ice
/î/	pierce
/o/	hot
/ō/	old
/ô/	song
/ôr/	fork
/oi/	oil
/ou/	out
/u/	up
/ū/	use
/ü/	rule
/u̇/	pull
/ûr/	turn
/ch/	chin
/ng/	sing
/sh/	shop
/th/	thin
/th/	this
/hw/	white
/zh/	treasure
/ə/	about
	taken
	pencil
	lemon
	circus

adj.	adjective
adv.	adverb
conj.	conjunction
contr.	contraction
def.	definition
interj.	interjection
n.	noun
pl.	plural
prep.	preposition
pron.	pronoun
sing.	singular
v.	verb
v.i.	intransitive verb
v.t.	transitive verb

slow /slō/ *adj.* **1.** not fast or quick. **2.** behind the correct time. **3.** not quick to learn or understand. **4.** not easily excited or moved. —*adv.* in a slow manner. —*v.* to make or become slow or slower. —**slow ly,** *adv.* —**slow ness,** *n.*

smile /smīl/ *n.* an expression of the face that is made by turning up the corners of the mouth. —*v.* **smiled, smil ing.** to have or give a smile.

smooth /smū<u>th</u>/ *adj.* **1.** having an even surface. **2.** even and gentle in movement. —*v.* **1.** to make even or level. **2.** to free from difficulty.

smudge /smuj/ *v.* **smudged, smudg ing.** to make or become dirty or smeared. —*n.* a dirty mark or stain.

snack /snak/ *n.* a small amount of food or drink eaten between regular meals.

snap /snap/ *v.* **snapped, snap ping.** **1.** to make or cause to make a sudden, sharp sound. **2.** to break suddenly and sharply. —*n.* **1.** a sudden, sharp, or breaking sound or action. **2.** a sudden bite or snatch. **3.** a short period of cold weather. **4.** a thin, crisp cookie.

sneak /snēk/ *v.* **sneaked** or **snuck, sneak ing.** to move, act, or take in a secret or sly way. *n.* a person who is sly and dishonest. *adj.* done, planned, or acting in a secret or sly manner.

snor kel /snôr ′ kəl/ *v.* **snor kel ing.** to swim using a snorkel.

soft /soft/ *adj.* **1.** easy to shape; not hard. **2.** smooth to the touch. **3.** gentle. **4.** kind. —*adv.* in a soft manner; gently. —**soft ly,** *adv.* —**soft ness,** *n.*

speak /spēk/ *v.* **spoke, spo ken, speak ing.** to use or utter words; talk.

speech /spēch/ *n., pl.* **speech es. 1.** the use of spoken words to express ideas, thoughts, and feelings. **2.** something that is spoken; talk. **3.** a way in which someone speaks.

spice /spīs/ *n.* **1.** the seeds or other parts of certain plants that are used to flavor food. **2.** something that adds interest or excitement. —*v.* **spiced, spic ing. 1.** to flavor with a spice or spices. **2.** to add interest or excitement to. —*adj.* **spic y.**

splotch /sploch/ *n., pl.* **splotch es.** a large, irregular spot; blot; stain. —*v.* to mark or cover with splotches. —**splotch y,** *adj.*

spruce /sprüs/ *n.* an evergreen

tree with drooping cones and short leaves shaped like needles.

square /skwâr/ *n.* a figure having four sides of equal length. —*adj.* **squar er, squar est.** having four equal sides. —*v.* **squared, squar ing. 1.** to make into the form of a right angle. **2.** to multiply a number by itself. —*adv.* directly and firmly.

squir rel /skwûr ′ əl/ *n.* a small animal with a long, bushy tail.

St. an abbreviation for *Street* used in a written address and for *Saint.*

stack /stak/ *n.* a number of things piled up one on top of the other; pile. —*v.* to pile or arrange in a stack.

stage /stāj/ *n.* **1.** a raised platform on which entertainers perform. **2.** a place where something important takes place. **3.** a single step, period, or degree in a process or development. **4.** a section of a rocket that has its own engine and fuel. It is usually separated from the rest of the rocket when its fuel is used up. —*v.* **staged, stag ing.** to plan, put on, or present.

starch /stärch/ *n., pl.* **starch es. 1.** a white food substance made and stored in most plants. Potatoes contain starch. **2.** a sub-stance used to make cloth stiff.

steal /stēl/ *v.* **stole, sto len, steal ing. 1.** to take something that does not belong to one. **2.** to get, take, or win by surprise or charm. **3.** to get to the next base in baseball without the help of a hit or error. —*n.* **1.** the act of stealing a base in baseball. **2.** something bought at a low price; bargain.

stock ing /stok ′ ing/ *n.* a snug, knitted covering for the foot and leg.

stoop [1] /stüp/ *n.* a small porch with stairs at the entrance of a house or other building.

stoop [2] /stüp/ *v.* **1.** to bend forward and downward. **2.** to lower or degrade oneself to do something. *I would never stoop to cheating.* —*n.* a bending forward of the head and shoulders.

stray /strā/ *n.* a lost or homeless animal. —*adj.* found here and there; scattered. —*v.* to wander away.

street /strēt/ *n.* a public way in a town or city, often with sidewalks and buildings on both sides.

stretch /strech/ *n., pl.* **stretch es. 1.** an unbroken space or area. **2.** the act of stretching. —*v.* to reach; extend.

/a/	at
/ā/	ape
/ä/	far
/â/	care
/e/	end
/ē/	me
/i/	it
/ī/	ice
/i/	pierce
/o/	hot
/ō/	old
/ô/	song
/ôr/	fork
/oi/	oil
/ou/	out
/u/	up
/ū/	use
/ü/	rule
/u̇/	pull
/ûr/	turn
/ch/	chin
/ng/	sing
/sh/	shop
/th/	thin
/th/	this
/hw/	white
/zh/	treasure
/ə/	about
	taken
	pencil
	lemon
	circus

adj.	adjective
adv.	adverb
conj.	conjunction
contr.	contraction
def.	definition
interj.	interjection
n.	noun
pl.	plural
prep.	preposition
pron.	pronoun
sing.	singular
v.	verb
v.i.	intransitive verb
v.t.	transitive verb

strike /strīk/ *v.* **struck, struck or strick en, strik ing.**
1. to give a blow to; hit. **2.** to set on fire by rubbing or hitting. **3.** to stop work in order to get an improvement or benefit. —*n.* **1.** the stopping of work. **2.** a sudden discovery. **3.** in baseball, a pitched ball that the batter swings at and misses or hits foul, or a pitched ball that passes through the strike zone.

style /stīl/ *n.* **1.** a particular way of saying or doing something. **2.** fashion.

sug ar /shùg ′ ər/ *n.* a white or brown sweet substance. Sugar comes from sugar beets and sugarcane.

suit /süt/ *n.* **1.** a set of clothes made to be worn together. **2.** a case brought to a court of law. **3.** any of the four sets of playing cards in a deck. —*v.* **1.** to meet the needs of. **2.** to be becoming to.

suit case /süt kās ′/ *n.* a flat bag for carrying clothes when traveling.

Sun. an abbreviation for *Sunday*.

sun set /sun ′ set ′/ *n.* the set-ting of the sun.

sup ply /sə plī ′/ *n.* a quantity of something that is needed or ready for use. —*v.* **sup plied, sup ply ing.** to provide with something needed or wanted.

sure /shùr/ *adj.* **1.** having no doubt; confident. **2.** steady; firm. —*adv.* **sure ly.** certainly.

sur face /sûr ′ fis/ *n.* **1.** the outside of a thing. **2.** outer look or appearance. —*adj.* of or having to do with a surface; on a surface. —*v.* **sur faced, sur fac ing. 1.** to come or rise to the surface. **2.** to cover the surface of.

sur prise /sər prīz ′, sûr prīz ′/ *v.* **sur prised, sur pris ing. 1.** to cause to feel sudden amazement. **2.** to find suddenly. —*n.* something that causes surprise.

swear /swâr/ *v.* **swore, sworn, swear ing.** to make a solemn statement. **2.** to say words that show hatred and anger; curse.

swim ming /swim ′ ing/ *n.* the act of a person or thing that swims. —*adj.* used for swimming or swimmers.

switch /swich/ *n., pl.* **switch es. 1.** a long, thin stick used for whipping. **2.** a device used to open or close an electric circuit. —*v.* **1.** to strike with a switch. **2.** to change. **3.** to turn on or off by means of an electric switch.

... T ....

tax /taks/ *n., pl.* **tax es.** money paid to the government by people or businesses. This money supports the government. —*v.* **1.** to put a tax on. **2.** to make a heavy demand on; strain.

term /tûrm/ *n.* **1.** a word or group of words that has a specific meaning. Serve *and* racket *are terms used in tennis.* **2.** a definite or limited period of time. **3. terms.** a relationship between people. **4.** a condition that is part of an agreement or a legal document. —*v.* to call or name.

thank ful /thangk ′ fəl/ *adj.* feeling or expressing thanks; grateful. —**thank ful ly,** *adv.* — **thank ful ness,** *n.*

thank less /thangk ′ lis/ *adj.* **1.** not likely to be rewarded or appreciated. **2.** not feeling or showing gratitude. —**thank less ly,** *adv.* —**thank ful ness,** *n.*

their /thâr/ *adj.* of, belonging to, or having to do with them.

them selves /them selvz ′, thəm selvz ′/ *pron.* **1.** their own selves. **2.** their usual, normal, or true selves.

there /thâr/ *adv.* **1.** at, in, or to that place. **2.** used to introduce a sentence in which a linking verb such as "be" comes before the subject. —*n.* that place. —*interj.* a word used to express satisfaction or sympathy.

there fore /thâr fôr ′/ *adv.* for that reason; as a result.

they're /thâr/ *contr.* shortened form of "they are."

thief /thēf/ *n., pl.* **thieves.** a person who steals.

thirst /thûrst/ *n.* **1.** an uncomfortable feeling of dryness in the mouth and throat. **2.** a strong desire or need for something.

thir teen /thûr ′ tēn/ *n., adj.* three more than ten; 13.

thir ty /thûr ′ tē/ *n., pl.* **thir ties.** *adj.* three times ten; 30.

though /thō/ *conj.* **1.** in spite of the fact that. **2.** but; yet; however. —*adv.* nevertheless, however.

thought ful /thôt ′ fəl/ *adj.* **1.** thinking. **2.** showing concern and care for others. —**thought ful ly,** *adv.* —**thought ful ness,** *n.*

through /thrü/ *prep.* **1.** from the beginning to the end of. **2.** in one side and out the other side of. **3.** in or to various places

/a/	at
/ā/	ape
/ä/	far
/â/	care
/e/	end
/ē/	me
/i/	it
/ī/	ice
/i/	pierce
/o/	hot
/ō/	old
/ô/	song
/ôr/	fork
/oi/	oil
/ou/	out
/u/	up
/ū/	use
/ü/	rule
/ù/	pull
/ûr/	turn
/ch/	chin
/ng/	sing
/sh/	shop
/th/	thin
/th/	this
/hw/	white
/zh/	treasure
/ə/	about
	taken
	pencil
	lemon
	circus

adj.	adjective
adv.	adverb
conj.	conjunction
contr.	contraction
def.	definition
interj.	interjection
n.	noun
pl.	plural
prep.	preposition
pron.	pronoun
sing.	singular
v.	verb
v.i.	intransitive verb
v.t.	transitive verb

in. **4.** in the midst of; among. **5.** because of. **6.** by means of. **7.** finished with; at the end of. —*adv.* from one side or end to the other side or end. —*adj.* **1.** allowing passage from one place to another with no obstruction. **2.** having reached a point of completion; finished.

throw /thrō/ *v.* **threw, thrown. 1.** to send up into or through the air. **2.** to make fall to the ground. **3.** to put or place suddenly in a certain position or condition.

Thurs. an abbreviation for *Thursday*.

tick et /tik ′ it/ *n.* a card or piece of paper that gives the person who holds it the right to be admitted or to get a service. —*v.* **1.** to attach a tag or label to. **2.** to give a traffic ticket to.

tight en /tī ′ tən/ *v.* to make or become tight or tighter.

to /tü, *unstressed* tu̇, tə/ *prep.* **1.** in the direction of; toward. **2.** on, upon, against.

too /tü/ *adv.* **1.** in addition to; also. **2.** very.

torch /tôrch/ *n., pl.* **torch es. 1.** a flaming light that can be carried in the hand. **2.** a tool that has a hot flame, used to

burn through or soften metal.

tow er /tow ər/ *n.* a tall, narrow building or structure. —*v.* to rise high up in the air.

trail /trāl/ *n.* **1.** a path through an area that is wild and not lived in. **2.** a mark, scent, or path made by a person or animal. —*v.* **1.** to follow behind. **2.** to follow the scent or path of.

train /trān/ *n.* **1.** a line of railroad cars connected together. **2.** a group of people, animals, or vehicles traveling together in a long line. **3.** a connected series of events, ideas, or parts. **4.** a part of a dress or robe that trails on the ground behind the person who wears it. —*v.* **1.** to teach, to behave, think, or grow up in a certain way. **2.** to teach how to do something. **3.** to get ready for something by practicing, exercising, or learning how. **4.** to make something grow or go in a certain way.

trick /trik/ *n.* **1.** a clever or skillful act. **2.** a joke or prank. —*v.* to fool or cheat with a trick.

tril lion /tril ′ yən/ *adj.* one followed by twelve zeros.

troop /trüp/ *n.* a group of persons or animals doing something together. —*v.* to walk or march in a group.

trou sers /trou ′ zərz/ *pl. n.* a

piece of clothing that reaches from the waist to the ankles and covers each leg separately; pants.

truck er /truk ′ ər/ *n.* a person whose job is driving a truck.

true /trü/ *adj.* **1.** agreeing with the facts. **2.** faithful; loyal. **3.** genuine; real.

Tues. an abbreviation for *Tuesday.*

tur tle /tûr ′ təl/ *n.* **1.** an animal with a low, wide body covered by a hard, rounded shell. **2.** a small triangle that appears on a computer monitor when the computer language LOGO is used.

twen ty /twen ′ tē/ *n., pl.* **twen ties.** *adj.* two times ten; 20.

twice /twīs/ *adj.* two times.

two /tü/ *n.* one more than one. *adj.* numbering more than one.

type /tīp/ *n.* **1.** a group of things that are alike or have the same qualities; kind. **2.** printed or type-written letters or numbers. —*v.* to write with a typewriter.

··· U ········ U ····

ug ly /ug ′ lē/ *adj.* **ug li er, ug li est.** **1.** not nice or pleasing

to look at. **2.** unpleasant; offensive. **3.** likely to cause trouble or harm. **4.** bad-tempered; cross.

um brel la /um brel ′ ə/ *n.* a circular piece of cloth or plastic stretched on a framework that can be folded up when not in use.

un- a prefix that means the opposite of; not. *Unexpected* means not expected.

un beat en /un bē ′ tən/ *adj.* **1.** never defeated or surpassed. **2.** not walked over. **3.** not shaped or mixed by beating.

un cov er /un kuv ′ ər/ *v.* **1.** to take away the cover from. **2.** to discover; make known.

un e qual /un ē ′ kwəl/ *adj.* **1.** not the same. **2.** not well matched.

un fair /un fâr ′/ *adj.* not fair or just.

un fin ished /un fin ′ isht/ *adj.* not finished.

un friend ly /un frend ′ lē/ *adj.* **un friend li er, un friend li est.** **1.** feeling or showing dislike; not friendly. **2.** not pleasant or favorable.

un hook /un hùk ′/ *v.* **1.** to remove from a hook. **2.** to unfasten the hooks of.

/a/	at
/ā/	ape
/ä/	far
/â/	care
/e/	end
/ē/	me
/i/	it
/ī/	ice
/î/	pierce
/o/	hot
/ō/	old
/ô/	song
/ôr/	fork
/oi/	oil
/ou/	out
/u/	up
/ū/	use
/ü/	rule
/ù/	pull
/ûr/	turn
/ch/	chin
/ng/	sing
/sh/	shop
/th/	thin
/th/	this
/hw/	white
/zh/	treasure
/ə/	about
	taken
	pencil
	lemon
	circus

141

adj. adjective
adv. adverb
conj. conjunction
contr. contraction
def. definition
interj. interjection
n. noun
pl. plural
prep. preposition
pron. pronoun
sing. singular
v. verb
v.i. intransitive verb
v.t. transitive verb

un paid /un pād ′/ *adj.* **1.** not yet paid. **2.** serving without pay; unsalaried.

un planned /un pland ′/ *adj.* not having a plan.

un safe /un sāf ′/ *adj.* not safe.

un seen /un sēn ′/ *adj.* not noticed or observed.

un tie /un tī ′/ *v.* **un tied, un ty ing.** to loosen or undo; set free.

urge /ûrj/ *v.* **urged, urg ing. 1.** to try to convince or persuade. **2.** to drive or force on.

use less /ūs ′ lis/ *adj.* serving no purpose; having no use. —**use less ly,** —**use less ness.**

va ca tion /vā kā ′ shən/ *n.* a period of rest or freedom from school, business, or other activity. —*v.* **va ca tion ing.** to take or spend a vacation.

val ue /val ′ ū/ *n.* **1.** the worth of something. —*v.* **val ued, val u ing. 1.** being worth an amount in money or exchange. **2.** think highly of.

view /vū/ *n.* **1.** something that is seen or can be seen. **2.** a particular way of thinking about something; opinion. —*v.* **1.** to look at or see. **2.** to think about or consider.

waist /wāst/ *n.* **1.** the part of the human body between the ribs and the hips. **2.** a piece of clothing or part of a piece of clothing that covers this part of the body.

wash /wôsh, wosh/ *v.* **1.** to make free of dirt by using soap and water. **2.** to carry away, wear away, or destroy by flowing water. —*n., pl.* **wash es.** the act of washing.

waste /wāst/ *v.* **wast ed, wast ing. 1.** to use or spend in a careless or useless way. **2.** to use up, wear away, or exhaust. **3.** to destroy; ruin. **4.** to lose energy, strength, or health slowly but steadily. —*n.* **1.** the act of wasting or the condition of being wasted. **2.** material that has been thrown away or is left over; refuse. **3.** material that has not been digested and is eliminated from the body.—*adj.* left over or worthless.

watch /woch/ *n., pl.* **watch es.**
1. the period of time when a person guards something.
2. a small device that measures and shows the time.
—*v.* **1.** to look at a person or thing carefully. **2.** to guard; take care of.

wa ter mel on /wô ′ tər mel ′ ən/ *n.* a large, juicy fruit that usually has a thick green outer covering.

wear /wâr/ *v.* **wore, worn, wear ing. 1.** to have on the body. **2.** to damage or reduce by long use or exposure.
—*n.* clothing.

Wed. an abbreviation for *Wednesday*.

weight /wāt/ *n.* **1.** the amount of heaviness of a person or thing. **2.** the quality of a thing that comes from the pull of gravity upon it. **3.** a burden or load. **4.** strong influence.

wheat /hwēt, wēt/ *n.* a kind of grass whose seeds are used to make flour and other foods.

whirl /hwûrl, wûrl/ *v.* to turn quickly in a circle. —*n.* a quick turn in a circle.

whole /hōl/ *adj.* having all its parts; entire; complete.
—*n.* all the parts that make up a thing.

whose /hüz/ *pron.* of or belonging to whom or which.

wid en /wī ′ dən/ *v.* to make or become wide or wider.

wife /wīf/ *n., pl.* **wives.** a married woman.

win dow /win ′ dō/ *n.* an opening in a wall or roof that lets in air and light.

wind y /win ′ dē/ *adj.* **wind i er, wind i est.** having or swept by strong winds.

wolf /wùlf/ *n., pl.* **wolves.** a wild animal that looks like a dog. Wolves have thick fur, a pointed muzzle, and a bushy tail.
—*v.* to eat very quickly and hungrily.

wom an /wùm ′ ən/ *n., pl.* **wo men. 1.** an adult female person. **2.** adult female people as a group.

wom en /wim ′ ən/ *pl. n.* plural of *woman*.

won der ful /wun ′ dər fəl/ *adj.* **1.** remarkable. **2.** very good; fine. —**won der ful ly,** *adv.* —**won der ful ness,** *n.*

wood en /wùd ′ ən/ *adj.* made of wood.

word /wûrd/ *n.* **1.** a sound or group of sounds having mean-

/a/	at
/ā/	ape
/ä/	far
/â/	care
/e/	end
/ē/	me
/i/	it
/ī/	ice
/î/	pierce
/o/	hot
/ō/	old
/ô/	song
/ôr/	fork
/oi/	oil
/ou/	out
/u/	up
/ū/	use
/ü/	rule
/ù/	pull
/ûr/	turn
/ch/	chin
/ng/	sing
/sh/	shop
/th/	thin
/th/	this
/hw/	white
/zh/	treasure
/ə/	about
	taken
	pencil
	lemon
	circus

adj.	adjective
adv.	adverb
conj.	conjunction
contr.	contraction
def.	definition
interj.	interjection
n.	noun
pl.	plural
prep.	preposition
pron.	pronoun
sing.	singular
v.	verb
v.i.	intransitive verb
v.t.	transitive verb

ing and forming a unit of a language. **2.** a written or printed letter or group of letters standing for such a sound. —*v.* to put into words.

work er /wûr ′ kər/ *n.* **1.** a person who works. **2.** a female insect who does most of the work in a colony.

world /wûrld/ *n.* **1.** the earth. **2.** a part of the earth. **3.** all the people who live on the earth.

worst /wûrst/ *adj.* **1.** most inferior; least good. **2.** most unfavorable. **3.** most harmful or severe. —*adv.* in the worst way. —*n.* something that is worst.

worth /wûrth/ *prep.* **1.** good enough for. **2.** having the same value as. **3.** having wealth that amounts to. —*n.* **1.** the quality that makes a thing good or useful. **2.** the value of something in money.

wreath /rēth/ *n., pl.* **wreaths** /rēthz or rēths/. a circle of leaves or flowers woven together.

wrench /rench/ *n., pl.* **wrench es. 1.** a very hard, sharp twist. *I gave the doorknob a wrench but the door was stuck.* **2.** a tool with jaws that is used to grip and turn a nut or bolt. —*v.* to twist or pull with a hard motion.

writ er /rī ′ tər/ *n.* a person who writes stories, poems, or articles; author.

··· **Y** ········· ····

yield /yēld/ *n.* an amount produced. —*v.* **1.** to produce. **2.** to give control or possession of to another. **3.** to stop fighting or disagreeing. **4.** to give way to force or pressure.

young /yung/ *adj.* in the early part of life or growth. —*n.* young offspring.

ANSWER KEY

ANSWER KEY

LESSON 1

Focus
page 2
1–6. scale, paper, brave, erase, male, paste
7–13. trail, brain, stray, grain, crayon, claim, railway
14–15. weight, freight
16–20. ch(a)mber, n(eigh)bor, b(a)sic, (a)gent, gl(a)cier

Words and Meanings
page 3
1. freight
2. railway
3. grain
4. paper
5. male
6. claim
7. trail
8. brave
9. brain
10. stray
11. scale
12. weight
13. crayon
14. erase
15. paste

Word Works
page 3
16. scaled, scaling
17. pasted, pasting
18. claimed, claiming
19. trailed, trailing
20. erased, erasing

Word Play
page 4
1–9. paper, erase, crayon, paste, freight, grain, scale, weight, railway

10. trail
11. scale
12. brave
13. male
14. paste
15. weight
16. stray
17. brain
18. erase
19. freight
20. claim

Write on Your Own
page 5
Journal entries will vary. Students should use at least four Core Words.

Check that students have used effective details.

The Write on Your Own activities need not always result in finished or published writing. Often it is more productive to focus on an aspect of good writing and have students experiment with various revisions without having them rewrite for submission and evaluation.

Proofreading Practice
page 5
1–4. stray, freight, brave, brain
5. home.
6. brain.

LESSON 2

Focus
page 6
1–8. east, sneak, grease, least, scream, wheat, seaw(ee)d, beach
9–13. field, donkey, jockey, yield, shield
14–16. bleed, seaweed, beetle
17–21. scr(ee)ch, f(e)male, wr(ea)th, n(ie)ce, m(ea)sles

Words and Meanings
page 7
1. east
2. beach
3. field
4. wheat
5. beetle
6. sneak
7. shield
8. jockey
9. donkey
10. yield
11. least
12. seaweed
13. grease
14. scream
15. bleed

Word Works
page 7
16. northeast
17. nosebleed
18. outfield
19. windshield
20. battlefield

Word Play
page 8
1. field
2. sneak
3. grease
4. scream
5. wheat
6. beach
7. least
8. beetle
9. bleed
10. jockey
11. seaweed
12. east
13. yield
14. donkey
15. shield

Write on Your Own
page 9
Letters will vary. Be sure students have included at least four Core Words. Check that students have used the correct forms for the salutations and complimentary closings.

Proofreading Practice
page 9
1–3. beach, seaweed, least
4. Jenny
5. Sunday

LESSON 3

Focus
page 10
1–9. flow, throw, shown, grown, hollow, narrow, window, bowl, shadow
10–12. grove, over, stolen
13–15. groan, coast, coach
16–20. bulld(o)zer, elb(ow), (o)verfl(ow), th(ough), c(o)c(oa)

Words and Meanings
page 11
1. coast
2. coach
3. grove
4. window
5. groan
6. over
7. narrow
8. throw
9. stolen
10. bowl
11. shown
12. hollow
13. grown
14. flow
15. shadow

Word Works
page 11
16–20. Sentences will vary.

Word Play
page 12
1. Hollow
2. Window
3. Throw
4. Coast
5. Coach
6. narrow
7. over
8. bowl
9. flow
10. coach
11–13. groan, grove, grown
14–16. shadow, shown, stolen

Write on Your Own
page 13
Story endings will vary. Be sure students have included at least four Core Words. Check that students have written surprising and creative conclusions for their stories.

Proofreading Practice
page 13
1–4. coach, shadow, hollow, stolen

LESSON 4

Focus
page 14
1–6. mild, find, blind, idle, pilot, pirate
7–10. flight, midnight, mighty, lighthouse
11–13. type, style, supply
14–15. pipeline, mile
16–20. h(y)drant, t(igh)ten, (i)cicle, rh(y)me, d(y)nam(i)te

Words and Meanings
page 15
1. pilot
2. mighty
3. midnight
4. idle
5. flight
6. find
7. pipeline
8. supply
9. lighthouse
10. pirate
11. mile
12. blind
13. type
14. style
15. mild

Word Works
page 15
16. retype, type again
17. reorder, order again
18. reclean, clean again
19. relock, lock again
20. remake, make again

Word Play
page 16
1. pipeline
2. midnight
3. pilot
4. lighthouse
5. mile
6. flight
7. pirate
8. find
9. type
10. mild
11. blind
12. style
13. supply
14. mighty
15. idle

Write on Your Own
page 17
Help wanted ads will vary. Be sure students have included at least four Core Words. Check that students have mentioned some of the things pilots must know and be able to do in their ads.

Proofreading Practice
page 17
1–4. pipeline, flight, type, supply

146

LESSON 5

Focus
page 18
1–4. move, proof, troop, stoop
5–6. drew, crew
7–13. rescue, due, suit, true, fruit, juice, bruise
14–15. few, view
16–20. gr(ou)p, sm(oo)th, val(ue), iss(ue), scr(ew)driver

Words and Meanings
page 19
1. stoop
2. true
3. move
4. fruit
5. juice
6. suit
7. proof
8. troop
9. view
10. few
11. rescue
12. crew
13. bruise
14. drew
15. due

Word Works
page 19
16. fearless
17. endless
18. thankless
19. clueless
20. careless

Word Play
page 20
1–2. rescue crew
3–4. fruit juice
5–6. true view
7. fruit
8. few
9. stoop
10. bruise
11. true
12. rescue
13. suit
14. move
15. view
16. due
17. troop
18. proof
19. drew
20. bruise

Write on Your Own
page 21
Interview questions will vary. Be sure students have included at least four Core Words. Check to make sure that students have used question marks appropriately.

Proofreading Practice
page 21
1–4. crew, bruise, true, rescue
5. working?
6. people?

LESSON 6

Focus
page 22
1–3. plow, allow, tower
4–8. found, ground, bounce, about, outside
9–12. joint, moist, choice, poison
13–15. destroy, employ, oyster
16–20. acc(ou)nt, app(oi)nt, enj(oy)ment, rej(oi)ce, tr(ou)sers

Words and Meanings
page 23
1. oyster
2. outside
3. ground
4. moist
5. poison
6. plow
7. found
8. employ
9. destroy
10. joint
11. allow
12. about
13. tower
14. bounce
15. choice

Word Works
page 23
16. allowing
17. poisoning
18. destroying
19. employing
20. plowing

Word Play
page 24
1. destroy
2. oyster
3. moist
4. ground
5. allow
6. plow
7. tower
8. choice
9. poison
10. bounce
11. joint
12. allow
13. outside
14. choice
15. found

Write on Your Own
page 25
Story endings will vary. Be sure students have included at least four Core Words. Check that students have used descriptive words to tell what happened to the oyster.

Proofreading Practice
page 25
1–4. found, ground, poison, moist
5. It climbed
6. The sun
7. Then it

LESSON 7

Focus
page 26
1–11. check, lucky, pocket, struck, bucket, hockey, attack, jacket, stocking, rocket, ticket
12–15. plastic, (picnic), attic, shriek
16–20. ni(ck)el, franti(c), heroi(c), atomi(c), poeti(c)

Words and Meanings
page 27
1. ticket
2. pocket
3. jacket
4. picnic
5. attic
6. attack
7. stocking
8. bucket
9. hockey
10. struck
11. shriek
12. rocket
13. plastic
14. lucky
15. check

Word Works
page 27
Answers may vary.
16. silly
17. angry
18. pretty
19. crabby
20. dizzy

Word Play
page 28
1. attic
2. jacket
3. bucket
4. rocket
5. hockey
6. check
7. rocket
8. struck
9. shriek
10. pocket
11. attack
12. lucky
13–14. jacket, stocking
15. hockey
16. attic
17. shriek
18. picnic
19. plastic
20. ticket

Write on Your Own
page 29
Newspaper ads will vary. Be sure students have included at least four Core Words. Check that students have used creative ways to convince buyers to come to the yard sale.

Proofreading Practice
page 29
1–4. ticket, plastic, picnic, bucket

LESSON 8

Focus
page 30
1–10. ceiling, citizen, (citrus), circle, cereal, celery, certain, cement, center, cedar
11–15. giraffe, gem, genius, gerbil, general
16–20. (c)entury, (c)ymbals, (g)enuine, (c)innamon, (g)eography

Words and Meanings
page 31
1. cedar
2. general
3. gerbil
4. gem
5. ceiling
6. center
7. certain
8. cement
9. genius
10. giraffe
11. citrus
12. celery
13. cereal
14. citizen
15. circle

Word Works
page 31
16. ceilings
17. circles
18. citizens
19. gems
20. gerbils

Word Play
page 32
1–2. giraffe, gerbil
3. citrus
4. cedar
5. general
6. citizen
7–8. cereal, celery
9. cement
10. ceiling
11. circle
12. gem
13–17. certain, citizen, citrus, genius, cedar
18. the middle point, part, or place of something
19. a main person, place, or thing
20. a main person, place, or thing

Write on Your Own
page 33
Stories will vary. Be sure students have included at least four Core Words. Check that students have used their imaginations to write about an invention that did not work.

Proofreading Practice
page 33
1–4. genius, certain, circle, ceiling
5. orders.
6. circle.

ANSWER KEY

LESSON 9

Focus
page 34
1–8. Dec., Nov., Jan., Apr., Feb., Oct., Aug., Mar.
9–15. Sat., Mon., Wed., Sun., Thurs., Tues., Fri.
16–20. (St.), (Blvd.), Sept., Ave., (Rd.)

Words and Meanings
page 35
1. Sat.
2. Jan.
3. Wed.
4. Feb.
5. Fri.
6. Mar.
7. Mon.
8. Apr.
9. Thurs.
10. Aug.
11. Tues.
12. Oct.
13. Sun.
14. Nov.
15. Dec.

Word Works
page 35
16. IL
17. MA
18. TX
19. MO
20. AZ
21. FL
22. KS
23. AK
24. NC

Word Play
page 36
1. Dec.
2. Mon.
3. Wed.
4. Oct.
5. Sun.
6. Fri.
7. Mar.
8. Sat.
9. Sun., Jan. 16
10. Mon., Aug. 24
11. Wed., Mar. 3
12. Tues., Feb. 16
13. Sat., Apr. 13
14. Thurs., Mar. 11
15. Jan.
16. Oct.
17. Nov.
18. Sun.
19. Apr.
20. Fri.

Write on Your Own
page 37
Charts will vary. Be sure students have included at least four Core Words. Check that students have used both capital letters and abbreviations for names of months and days.

Proofreading Practice
page 37
1–6. Jan., Apr., Mon., Tues., Wed., Thurs.

LESSON 10

Focus
page 38
1–8. ranch, pinch, perch, torch, reach, couch, branch, church
9–15. stretch, scratch, sketch, clutch, hutch, patch, watch
16–20. star(ch), cin(ch), pa(tch)work, wren(ch), splo(tch)

Words and Meanings
page 39
1. stretch
2. torch
3. scratch
4. ranch
5. hutch
6. watch
7. couch
8. sketch
9. clutch
10. church
11. reach
12. pinch
13. perch
14. branch
15. patch

Word Works
page 39
16. ranches
17. perches
18. torches
19. watches
20. sketches

Word Play
page 40
1. couch
2. ranch
3. branch
4. torch
5. hutch
6. sketch
7. watch
8. patch
9. church
10. pinch
11. perch
12. stretch
13. reach
14. scratch
15. clutch

Write on Your Own
page 41
Letters will vary. Be sure students have included at least four Core Words. Check that students have used words like *first, next, after that,* and *then* correctly in their letters.

Proofreading Practice
page 41
1–4. ranch, branch, reach, church

LESSON 11

Focus
page 42
1–6. dollars, suitcases, monkeys, eagles, bicycles, umbrellas
7–13. taxes, ashes, crutches, inches, sandwiches, brushes, radishes
14–15. countries, blueberries
16–20. relish(es), galler(ies), smudge(s), dragonfl(ies), marsh(es)

Words and Meanings
page 43
1. bicycles
2. countries
3. monkeys
4. eagles
5. taxes
6. dollars
7. inches
8. crutches
9. brushes
10. ashes
11. suitcases
12. umbrellas
13. sandwiches
14. radishes
15. blueberries

Word Works
page 43
16. happens every two months
17. speaks two languages
18. for use with two eyes
19. happens every two weeks
20. cut into two parts

Word Play
page 44
1. dollars
2. blueberries
3. monkeys
4. brushes
5. radishes
6. eagles
7. bicycles
8. countries
9. crutches
10. ashes
11. suitcases
12–13. suitcases, blueberries
14–15. umbrellas, blueberries
16. sandwiches
17. blueberries
18. countries
19. noun, verb
20. noun, verb
21. noun
22. noun, verb

Write on Your Own
page 45
Journal entries will vary. Be sure students have included at least four Core Words. Check for the use of descriptive words.

Proofreading Practice
page 45
1–4. dollars, monkeys, eagles, sandwiches
5. Today
6. We brought

LESSON 12

Focus**
page 46
1–6. chan(c)e, pri(c)e, prin(c)e, twi(c)e, (s)pi(c)e, (s)pru(c)e
7–15. noti(c)e, (s)enten(c)e, re(c)e(ss), (s)urfa(c)e, prin(c)e(ss), offi(c)e, i(c)eberg, advi(c)e, fau(c)et
16–20. devi(c)e, (sc)ien(c)e, crevi(c)e, in(s)tan(c)e, di(s)tan(c)e

Words and Meanings
page 47
1. price
2. spice
3. chance
4. twice
5. iceberg
6. faucet
7. surface
8. spruce
9. advice
10. recess
11. prince
12. princess
13. office
14. notice
15. sentence

Word Works
page 47
16. the prince's hat
17. the pony's neck
18. the helper's job
19. the boat's side
20. the castle's gate

Word Play
page 48
1. twice
2. iceberg
3. faucet
4. recess
5. spruce
6. surface
7. prince
8–15. advice, prince, sentence, spice, office, twice, princess, notice
16. chance
17. twice
18. spice
19. advice
20. price

Write on Your Own
page 49
Stories will vary. Be sure students have included at least four Core Words. Check that students have written an appropriate beginning, middle, and conclusion for their stories.

Proofreading Practice
page 49
1–4. iceberg, surface, office, advice

148

LESSON 13

Focus
page 50

1–6. term, heard, learn, serve, pearl, early

7–11. birth, burst, thirst, urge, further

12–15. word, world, worst, worth

16–20. s(ear)ch, p(ur)pose, p(er)fect, (ear)nest, overh(ear)d

Words and Meanings
page 51

1. urge
2. early
3. birth
4. learn
5. word
6. thirst
7. world
8. worth
9. pearl
10. burst
11. further
12. serve
13. term
14. worst
15. heard

Word Works
page 51

16. wordy
17. watery
18. thirsty
19. pearly
20. spicy

Word Play
page 52

1. heard
2. learn
3. thirst
4. urge
5. further
6. burst
7. birth
8. serve
9. early
10. worth
11. word
12. term
13. early
14. serve
15. learn
16. pearl
17. worth
18. world
19. serve
20. worst

Write on Your Own
page 53

Descriptions will vary. Be sure students have included at least four Core Words. Check the stories for creativity.

Proofreading Practice
page 53

1–4. pearl, worth, world, serve

LESSON 14

Focus
page 54

1–5. hungry, happy, pretty, ugly, heavy

6–10. prettier, uglier, happier, heavier, hungrier

11–15. heaviest, prettiest, hungriest, ugliest, happiest

16–20. empt(y), gloom(y), wind(y), health(y), chill(y)

Words and Meanings
page 55

1. heavy
2. heavier
3. heaviest
4. hungry
5. hungrier
6. hungriest
7. pretty
8. prettiest
9. prettier
10. happy
11. happiest
12. happier
13. ugly
14. uglier
15. ugliest

Word Works
page 55

16. rainier, rainiest
17. sunnier, sunniest
18. snowier, snowiest
19. cloudier, cloudiest
20. funnier, funniest

Word Play
page 56

1. happy
2. prettiest
3. heaviest
4. happier
5. uglier
6. heavy
7. ugly
8. heavier
9. ugliest
10. hungry
11. happy
12. hungriest
13. happier
14. pretty
15. hungrier
16. happiest
17. prettier

Write on Your Own
page 57

Journal entries will vary. Be sure students have included at least four Core Words. Check that students have used descriptive words to tell about a day they spent exploring in the jungle.

Proofreading Practice
page 57

1–4. ugly, prettier, heaviest, hungriest
5. fighting.
6. heaviest.

LESSON 15

Focus
page 58

1–7. loaf, scarf, wife, thief, shelf, wolf, leaf

8–15. leaves, wolves, themselves, wives, shelves, thieves, scarves, loaves

16–20. geese, (dominoes) women, (skis), oxen

Words and Meanings
page 59

1. loaf
2. shelf
3. shelves
4. loaves
5. leaf
6. themselves
7. wolves
8. thieves
9. scarves
10. wife
11. wolf
12. thief
13. wives
14. leaves
15. scarf

Word Works
page 59

16. cacti
17. children
18. teeth
19. men
20. mice

Word Play
page 60

1. scarf
2. thieves
3. wife
4. shelf
5. leaf
6. themselves
7. loaf
8. wolf
9. leaves
10. scarves
11. loaves
12. wolves
13. scarves
14. loaf
15. shelves
16. wolves
17. wives
18. thief

Write on Your Own
page 61

Story endings will vary. Be sure students have included at least four Core Words. Check that students have written about what happened to the elf at the end of the story.

Proofreading Practice
page 61

1–4. leaves, wolves, wolf, loaves

LESSON 16

Focus
page 62

1–8. review, reappear, rewind, remove, rename, retake, replace, rearrange

9–15. unfriendly, untie, unhook, unpaid, unfair, uncover, unbeaten

16–20. (un)planned, (re)finish, (un)finished, (re)verse, (un)equal

Words and Meanings
page 63

1. reappear
2. replace
3. uncover
4. rearrange
5. remove
6. unbeaten
7. unfriendly
8. unpaid
9. unhook
10. untie
11. rewind
12. retake
13. unfair
14. rename
15. review

Word Works
page 63

16. uncommon
17. rejoin
18. unlike
19. rewrite
20. unhappy

Word Play
page 64

1–5. unfriendly, reappear, uncover, rearrange, unbeaten
6–7. reappear, rearrange
8–12. rename, unpaid, retake, unfair, replace
13–17. retake, reappear, unhook, unfair, rewind
18. unfriendly
19. untie
20. review
21. remove
22. unbeaten
23. rearrange
24. replace

Write on Your Own
page 65

Newspaper reviews will vary. Be sure students have included at least four Core Words. Check that students have written appropriate headlines for their reviews.

Proofreading Practice
page 65

1–4. unfriendly, reappear, untie, remove

ANSWER KEY

149

A N S W E R   K E Y

LESSON 17

Focus
page 66
1–15. forth, fourth; flour, flower; (their) (there), they're; foul, fowl; threw, through; miner, minor; waste, waist
16–20. pour, pore, poor; principal, principle

Words and Meanings
page 67
1. foul
2. fowl
3. forth
4. fourth
5. there
6. their
7. they're
8. threw
9. minor
10. miner
11. through
12. flower
13. waste
14. flour
15. waist

Word Works
page 67
16. who's
17. your
18. Whose
19. you're
20. Here's

Word Play
page 68
1–2. (threw), through
3–4. (flour), flower
5–7. (their), there, they're
8. miner
9. minor
10. waist
11. waste
12. fowl
13. foul
14. forth
15. fourth
16. waist
17. flower
18. fourth

Write on Your Own
page 69
Letters will vary. Be sure students have included at least four Core Words. Check that students have used their imaginations to come up with creative ways to help the farmer.

Proofreading Practice
page 69
1–4. fowl, there, waste, their

LESSON 18

Focus
page 70
1–7. woman, even, kitten, open, happen, garden, problem
8–15. bottom, custom, person, reason, lesson, button, cannon, ribbon
16–20. horiz(o)n, crims(o)n, watermel(o)n, drag(o)n, opini(o)n

Words and Meanings
page 71
1. happen
2. custom
3. person
4. open
5. button
6. ribbon
7. bottom
8. reason
9. even
10. kitten
11. problem
12. garden
13. cannon
14. lesson
15. woman

Word Works
page 71
16. mit/ten
17. sor/row
18. ad/dress
19. mil/lion
20. es/say

Word Play
page 72
1. button
2. lesson
3. garden
4. kitten
5–11. kitten, bottom, happen, lesson, button, cannon, ribbon
12–14. person, reason, lesson
15. woman
16. problem
17–19. even, open, reason
20. cus/tom
21. o/pen
22. rea/son
23. prob/lem

Write on Your Own
page 73
Paragraphs will vary. Be sure students have included at least four Core Words. Check that students have used descriptive words to tell how they felt on a particular day.

Proofreading Practice
page 73
1–4. woman, garden, kitten, button
5. The
6. She

LESSON 19

Focus
page 74
1–8. action, nation, motion, mention, caution, location, condition, direction
9–14. picture, creature, nature, furniture, feature, posture
15. failure
16–20. atten(tion), lec(ture), depar(ture), crea(tion), mois(ture)

Words and Meanings
page 75
1. creature
2. nature
3. furniture
4. nation
5. direction
6. picture
7. posture
8. motion
9. action
10. caution
11. mention
12. location
13. condition
14. feature
15. failure

Word Works
page 75
16. natural
17. national
18. conditional
19. regional
20. practical

Word Play
page 76
1. motion
2. mention
3. action
4. creature
5. posture
6. feature
7. caution
8. nature
9. nation
10. failure
11. motion
12. nature
13. nation
14. furniture
15. direction
16. condition
17. location
18. picture

Write on Your Own
page 77
Story endings will vary. Be sure students have included at least four Core Words. Check that students have followed the steps on pages 134–135 to help them with the writing process.

Proofreading Practice
page 77
1–4. direction, failure, creature, action
5. Dragonking
6. year I

LESSON 20

Focus
page 78
1–7. eighteen, thirteen, nineteen, fifteen, sixteen, seventeen, fourteen
8–11. twenty, ninety, fifty, forty
12–13. fifth, eighth
14–15. hundred, million
16–20. (numeral), digit, arithmetic, (decimal), trillion

Words and Meanings
page 79
1. fifth
2. eighth
3. thirteen
4. fourteen
5. fifteen
6. sixteen
7. seventeen
8. eighteen
9. nineteen
10. twenty
11. forty
12. fifty
13. ninety
14. hundred
15. million

Word Works
page 79
16. fifteenth
17. hundredth
18. fiftieth
19. millionth
20. fortieth

Word Play
page 80
1–9. eighth, forty, fifty, seventeen, fourteen, twenty, fifteen, fifth, million
10. thirteen
11. hundred
12. fourteen
13. ninety
14. eighteen
15. sixteen
16. twenty
17. seventeen
18. nineteen
19. fifty

Write on Your Own
page 81
Poems will vary. Be sure students have included at least four Core Words. Check that students have used ordinal and cardinal numbers correctly in their poems.

Proofreading Practice
page 81
1–4. nineteen, twenty, forty, fifty

ANSWER KEY

LESSON 21

Focus
page 82
Circled elements will vary.
1–7. sh(oe), y(ou)ng, (s)ure, (gu)ess, fr(o)nt, w(a)sh, (wh)ose
8–14. ans(w)er, (s)ug(ar), ob(ey), c(ou)sin, o(cea)n, of(t)en, i(s)land
15. (a)n(o)ther
16–20. h(ea)rt, ma(ch)ine, ag(ai)nst, b(eau)ty, h(eigh)t

Words and Meanings
page 83
1. island
2. ocean
3. cousin
4. another
5. sure
6. often
7. shoe
8. wash
9. young
10. whose
11. obey
12. sugar
13. answer
14. front
15. guess

Word Works
page 83
Sentences will vary
16. disappear
17. displease
18. disobey
19. distrust
20. disagree
21. dishonest
22. disproves

Word Play
page 84
1. island
2. ocean
3. cousin
4. answer
5. obey
6. guess
7. young
8. shoe
9. wash
10. ocean
11. sure
12. front
13. sugar
14–17. island, often, guess, answer
18–20. obey, ocean, often
21–23. shoe, sugar, sure
24–26. wash, whose, young
27–30. another, answer, ocean, often

Write on Your Own
page 85
Help wanted ads will vary. Be sure students have included at least four Core Words. Check that students have described what the job on the farm will be like.

Proofreading Practice
page 85
1–4. young, ocean, answer, sure

LESSON 22

Focus
page 86
1–10. glare, daring, area, scare, library, beware, carry, compare, declare, narrate
11–15. despair, swear, therefore, repair, dairy
16–20. prep(are), comp(ar)ison, cl(ar)ify, b(ur)y, l(ar)iat

Words and Meanings
page 87
1. beware
2. declare
3. glare
4. scare
5. area
6. swear
7. compare
8. Therefore
9. daring
10. narrate
11. dairy
12. carry
13. library
14. despair
15. repair

Word Works
page 87
16. scares
17. scared
18. scaring
19. scary
20. scarier
21. scariest
22. scariness

Word Play
page 88
1–3. glare, scare, swear
4–5. carry, narrate
6–8. library, carry, dairy
9. dairy
10. library
11. repair
12. beware
13. scare
14. glare
15. area
16. swear
17. narrate
18. compare
19. dare
20. declare
21–25. area, library, therefore, glare, despair

Write on Your Own
page 89
Newspaper articles will vary. Be sure students have included at least four Core Words. Check that students have written short headlines for their articles.

Proofreading Practice
page 89
1–4. area, daring, Beware, scare
5. daring.
6. food.

LESSON 23

Focus
page 90
1–9. joyful, thankful, careful, hopeful, harmful, fearful, painful, playful, skillful
10–15. useless, homeless, helpless, painless, cloudless, thankless
16–20. powerful, wonderful, breathless, respectful, thoughtful

Words and Meanings
page 91
1. cloudless
2. thankful
3. fearful
4. careful
5. painful
6. useless
7. helpless
8. painless
9. harmful
10. thankless
11. playful
12. skillful
13. hopeful
14. homeless
15. joyful

Word Works
page 91
16. fearless
17. thankful
18. colorful
19. cheerlessly
20. hopefully

Word Play
page 92
1–6. joyful, careful, hopeful, harmful, fearful, playful
7–8. painless, painful
9–10. thankful, thankless
11. helpless
12. cloudless
13–14. hopeful, homeless
15. careful
16. skillful
17. panic
18. play
19. homeless

Write on Your Own
page 93
Rules will vary. Be sure students have included at least four Core Words. Check that students have used parallel sentence structures.

Proofreading Practice
page 93
1–4. harmful, careful, useless, playful

LESSON 24

Focus
page 94
1–6. going, building, relaxing, climbing, reading, skiing
7–10. dancing, exploring, biking, riding
11–15. swimming, napping, snapping, flipping, jogging
16–20. (breathing), snorkeling, (practicing), vacationing, (exercising)

Words and Meanings
page 95
1. going
2. relaxing
3. swimming
4. flipping
5. snapping
6. climbing
7. skiing
8. exploring
9. riding
10. biking
11. jogging
12. dancing
13. reading
14. napping
15. building

Word Works
page 95
16. surfer
17. golfed
18. bowler
19. explores
20. flipped

Word Play
page 96
1. Biking
2. Reading
3. Skiing
4. Riding
5. Swimming
6. Jogging
7–9. snapping, flipping, climbing
10. exploring
11–12. napping, relaxing
13. building
14. going
15. dancing

Write on Your Own
page 97
Letters will vary. Be sure students have included at least four Core Words. Check that students have used the correct forms for the salutations and complimentary closings.

Proofreading Practice
page 97
1–4. swimming, biking, building, riding
5. July
6. castles.

ANSWER KEY

REVIEW 1-4

1. scale
2. grain
3. brain
4. crayon
5. wheat
6. east
7. beetle
8. bleed
9. hollow
10. narrow
11. coast
12. throw
13. mile
14. idle
15. midnight
16. blind

REVIEW 5-8

1. true
2. fruit
3. few
4. due
5. moist
6. outside
7. found
8. allow
9. attack
10. shriek
11. rocket
12. picnic
13. giraffe
14. cereal
15. circle
16. ceiling

REVIEW 9-12

1. Tues. /Dec.
2. Aug.
3. Wed.
4. Sun. /Nov.
5. perch
6. scratch
7. sketch
8. couch
9. brushes
10. dollars
11. countries
12. inches
13. advice
14. twice
15. price
16. surface

REVIEW 13-16

1. early
2. birth
3. worst
4. further
5. hungrier
6. prettiest
7. ugliest
8. happiest
9. loaf
10. wolves
11. thief
12. leaves
13. rearrange
14. unfair
15. untie
16. review

REVIEW 17-20

1. fowl
2. fourth
3. flower
4. waist
5. Open
6. woman
7. garden
8. ribbon
9. furniture
10. nation
11. failure
12. direction
13. fourteen
14. ninety
15. fifth
16. eighth

REVIEW 21-24

1. sure
2. obey
3. ocean
4. shoe
5. Beware
6. library
7. swear
8. despair
9. cloudless
10. fearful
11. careful
12. helpless
13. skiing
14. napping
15. exploring
16. biking

ANSWER

KEY

BASIC SKILLS BUILDER K to 2 – THE MAGIC APPLEHOUSE

At the Magic Applehouse, children discover that Abigail Appleseed runs a deliciously successful business selling apple pies, tarts, and other apple treats. Enthusiasm grows as children join in the fun of helping Abigail run her business. Along the way they'll develop computer and entrepreneurial skills to last a lifetime. They will run their own business – all while they're having bushels of fun!

TITLE	ISBN	PRICE
Basic Skills Builder –The Magic Applehouse	1-57768-312-9	$9.95

Available in jewel case only (no box included)

TEST PREP – SCORING HIGH

This grade-based testing software will help prepare your child for standardized achievement tests given by his or her school. Scoring High specifically targets the skills required for success on the Stanford Achievement Test (SAT) for grades three through eight. Lessons and test questions follow the same format and cover the same content areas as questions appearing on the actual SAT tests. The practice tests are modeled after the SAT test-taking experience with similar directions, number of questions per section, and bubble-sheet answer choices.

Scoring High is a child's first-class ticket to a winning score on standardized achievement tests!

TITLE	ISBN	PRICE
Grades 3 to 5: Scoring High Test Prep	1-57768-316-1	$9.95
Grades 6 to 8: Scoring High Test Prep	1-57768-317-X	$9.95

Available in jewel case only (no box included)

SCIENCE

Mastering the principles of both physical and life science has never been so FUN for kids grades six and above as it is while they are exploring McGraw-Hill's edutainment software!

TITLE	ISBN	PRICE
Grades 6 & up: Life Science	1-57768-336-6	$9.95
Grades 8 & up: Physical Science	1-57768-308-0	$9.95

Available in jewel case only (no box included)

REFERENCE

The National Museum of Women in the Arts has teamed with McGraw-Hill Consumer Products to bring you this superb collection available for your enjoyment on CD-ROM.

This special collection is a visual diary of 200 women artists from the Renaissance to the present, spanning 500 years of creativity.

You will discover the art of women who excelled in all the great art movements of history. Artists who pushed the boundaries of abstract, genre, landscape, narrative, portrait, and still-life styles; as well as artists forced to push the societal limits placed on women through the ages.

TITLE	ISBN	PRICE
Women in the Arts	1-57768-010-3	$29.95

Available in boxed version only

Visit us on the Internet at:

www.MHkids.com

Most software titles for Windows 3.1™, Windows '95™ & '98™, and Macintosh™.

Or call 800-298-4119 for your local retailer.

All our workbooks meet school curriculum guidelines and correspond to
The McGraw-Hill Companies classroom textbooks.

SPECTRUM SERIES

DOLCH Sight Word Activities

The DOLCH Sight Word Activities Workbooks use the classic Dolch list of 220 basic vocabulary words that make up from 50% to 75% of all reading matter that children ordinarily encounter. Since these words are ordinarily recognized on sight, they are called *sight words*. Volume 1 includes 110 sight words. Volume 2 covers the remainder of the list. Over 160 pages.

TITLE	ISBN	PRICE
Grades K-1 Vol. 1	1-57768-429-X	$9.95
Grades K-1 Vol. 2	1-57768-439-7	$9.95

GEOGRAPHY

Full-color, three-part lessons strengthen geography knowledge and map reading skills. Focusing on five geographic themes including location, place, human/environmental interaction, movement, and regions. Over 150 pages. Glossary of geographical terms and answer key included.

TITLE	ISBN	PRICE
Gr 3, Communities	1-57768-153-3	$7.95
Gr 4, Regions	1-57768-154-1	$7.95
Gr 5, USA	1-57768-155-X	$7.95
Gr 6, World	1-57768-156-8	$7.95

MATH

Features easy-to-follow instructions that give students a clear path to success. This series has comprehensive coverage of the basic skills, helping children to master math fundamentals. Over 150 pages. Answer key included.

PHONICS

Provides everything children need to build multiple skills in language. Focusing on phonics, structural analysis, and dictionary skills, this series also offers creative ideas for using phonics and word study skills in other language arts. Over 200 pages. Answer key included.

TITLE	ISBN	PRICE
Grade 1	1-57768-111-8	$7.95
Grade 2	1-57768-112-6	$7.95
Grade 3	1-57768-113-4	$7.95
Grade 4	1-57768-114-2	$7.95
Grade 5	1-57768-115-0	$7.95
Grade 6	1-57768-116-9	$7.95
Grade 7	1-57768-117-7	$7.95
Grade 8	1-57768-118-5	$7.95

TITLE	ISBN	PRICE
Grade K	1-57768-120-7	$7.95
Grade 1	1-57768-121-5	$7.95
Grade 2	1-57768-122-3	$7.95
Grade 3	1-57768-123-1	$7.95
Grade 4	1-57768-124-X	$7.95
Grade 5	1-57768-125-8	$7.95
Grade 6	1-57768-126-6	$7.95

READING

This full-color series creates an enjoyable reading environment, even for below-average readers. Each book contains captivating content, colorful characters, and compelling illustrations, so children are eager to find out what happens next. Over 150 pages. Answer key included.

TITLE	ISBN	PRICE
Grade K	1-57768-130-4	$7.95
Grade 1	1-57768-131-2	$7.95
Grade 2	1-57768-132-0	$7.95
Grade 3	1-57768-133-9	$7.95
Grade 4	1-57768-134-7	$7.95
Grade 5	1-57768-135-5	$7.95
Grade 6	1-57768-136-3	$7.95

SPELLING

This full-color series links spelling to reading and writing and increases skills in words and meanings, consonant and vowel spellings, and proofreading practice. Over 200 pages. Speller dictionary and answer key included.

TITLE	ISBN	PRICE
Grade 1	1-57768-161-4	$7.95
Grade 2	1-57768-162-2	$7.95
Grade 3	1-57768-163-0	$7.95
Grade 4	1-57768-164-9	$7.95
Grade 5	1-57768-165-7	$7.95
Grade 6	1-57768-166-5	$7.95

WRITING

Lessons focus on creative and expository writing using clearly stated objectives and pre-writing exercises. Eight essential reading skills are applied. Activities include main idea, sequence, comparison, detail, fact and opinion, cause and effect, and making a point. Over 130 pages. Answer key included.

TITLE	ISBN	PRICE
Grade 1	1-57768-141-X	$7.95
Grade 2	1-57768-142-8	$7.95
Grade 3	1-57768-143-6	$7.95
Grade 4	1-57768-144-4	$7.95
Grade 5	1-57768-145-2	$7.95
Grade 6	1-57768-146-0	$7.95
Grade 7	1-57768-147-9	$7.95
Grade 8	1-57768-148-7	$7.95

TEST PREP
From the Nation's #1 Testing Company

Prepares children to do their best on current editions of the five major standardized tests. Activities reinforce test-taking skills through examples, tips, practice, and timed exercises. Subjects include reading, math, and language. Over 150 pages. Answer key included.

TITLE	ISBN	PRICE
Grade 1	1-57768-101-0	$8.95
Grade 2	1-57768-102-9	$8.95
Grade 3	1-57768-103-7	$8.95
Grade 4	1-57768-104-5	$8.95
Grade 5	1-57768-105-3	$8.95
Grade 6	1-57768-106-1	$8.95
Grade 7	1-57768-107-X	$8.95
Grade 8	1-57768-108-8	$8.95

LANGUAGE ARTS

Encourages creativity and builds confidence by making writing fun! Seventy-two four-part lessons strengthen writing skills by focusing on parts of speech, word usage, sentence structure, punctuation, and proofreading. Each level includes a *Writer's Handbook* at the end of the book that offers writing tips. This series is based on the highly respected SRA/McGraw-Hill language arts series. More than 180 full-color pages.

TITLE	ISBN	PRICE
Grade 2	1-57768-472-9	$7.95
Grade 3	1-57768-473-7	$7.95
Grade 4	1-57768-474-5	$7.95
Grade 5	1-57768-475-3	$7.95
Grade 6	1-57768-476-1	$7.95